Finding Our Purpose in Life: A Step-by-Step Method

Opening Up to Your Core

By

J. Travers Hartnett

Shaw Street Media
1045 E. Atlantic Ave #203
Delray Beach, Fl 33483

www.shawstreetmedia.com

ISBN: 978-0-9853676-0-2

Although the author and publisher have made every effort to ensure that the information in this book was correct at press time, the author and publisher do not assume and hereby disclaim any liability to any party for any loss, damage, or disruption caused by errors or omissions, whether such errors or omissions result from negligence, accident, or any other cause.

This book is not intended as a substitute for the medical advice of physicians. The reader should regularly consult a physician in matters relating to his/her health and particularly with respect to any symptoms that may require diagnosis or medical attention.

Graphic chart design provided by Antonina Guarino

Printed in the United States of America

CONTENTS

Introduction

Chapter I:
A Beautiful, Blended Mind

3

Chapter 2:
Getting Organized

Chapter 3:
About Dreams

Chapter 4:
Your Sweet Personal Dreams

Chapter 5:
Reviewing Dreams for Awareness, Suggestions and Prophecies

Chapter 6:
Tough Decisions

Chapter 7:
Heroes and Role Models

Chapter 8:
People I Avoid

Chapter 9:
Reinforcing and Bridging to Resolve Conflicts

Chapter 10:
Opening Up to Your Conscience

Introduction

An Accidental Journey

One early morning in late October 2003, I woke up singing a vaguely familiar song. I was still half asleep. All I could remember was the fading, repetitive lyric question, "have you ever seen the rain, have you ever seen the rain, have you ever seen the rain?" The name of the song and why I woke up singing it were a mystery. It was only days later I remembered a song by the same name, Have You Ever Seen the Rain, performed by Creedence Clearwater Revival (CCR). I went on the Internet and looked up the lyrics. They were not very upbeat.

At the time, I knew I was in big health trouble, but I didn't pay much attention to the message. Besides, I liked the tune. You see, I had had a long history of neck problems. It started with three operations before my teen years, and then I underwent a double laminectomy surgery, which opened up my cervical spinal cord to prevent my mobility problems from getting worse. I had no idea I had just received my first prophecy dream, and the message wasn't good.

I discovered years later that my major and minor occipital nerves had become encapsulated within my new surgical scar tissue, and they were now hard as cement." I was in bigger trouble than I realized. These sensory nerves, located in the back of my neck, are hardwired to the base of the brain. Every time I moved my head, bent down, or took a walk, these nerves were yanked, resulting in what I called "lie on the floor" headaches. I could walk around, but there was always the price of head and neck pain. Sleep was a break from my growing discomfort, and unlike a child, I always looked forward to my bedtime.

Waking Dream Songs from the Unconscious

For many months before I experienced my first dream song, I had kept a pain journal in an attempt to maintain control over my growing discomfort and to better describe what was going on to my doctor. Three times a day, I documented my pain from 1–10 for intensity, and I noted the site of the pain. I gave my pain locations names such as "the temple hook," "sharp jaw," "top spot," "band of steel," and "pulsars." The journal also included everything I had done to get through the day. This included the number of hot showers, hot pads, ice packs, and naps taken as well as my ever-changing emotions. It took me years to figure out I was receiving these waking songs because my unconscious was reading my pain journal as I wrote it.

Ever since hearing my first dream song, I have awoken almost every day to lyrics from a different song. I keep a pad next to my bed so I can write down the words I remember when I wake up. I always get excited to search for the new song on the Internet. Some lyrics even come from tunes that were popular before I was born. Other songs are more recent, including a lot of music I didn't appreciate when first released. I now love these songs not just for their messages but also for my newfound discovery of the recording artists. I try to place the songs in the history of my life and guess where I heard them first.

Five years ago, I took a training course in hypnotherapy in Ft. Lauderdale, Florida. I mentioned my waking songs to my instructor and explained they were becoming more frequent and vivid while taking her course.

"That's good," she said. "That means you are opening up."

Because "opening up" sounded like a good thing, I was pleased. I assumed she meant I was getting more in touch with my feelings. I have since learned the expression "opening up" has an entirely different meaning. It meant I was consciously receiving information from my unconscious, which was actively communicating with me by these dream songs. It was also obvious these songs were trying to warn and console me. I found out later that this type of communication with your unconscious is unusual. Normally there are only two ways we receive conscious messages from the unconscious: by our dreams or by our imaginations bubbling up into our thoughts. "Waking songs" from the unconscious are very unusual. Maybe my past attempts at writing music contributed to this amazing phenomenon.

I kept receiving new songs almost every day. Over time, however, I started to become concerned. While the songs' messages were always supportive, insightful, and great fun to research, I was becoming increasingly alarmed. Exactly where were they coming from? Exactly *who* was choosing these songs and sending them to me? This question led me to do extensive research on how we communicate with the unconscious, and it ultimately compelled me to write this book and share my opening up methodology. It was only by opening up that I discovered my own purpose in life.

The God to Man Connection

Years ago, when I was a small child, my mother told me in her gentle voice that God especially loves those who suffer. She said he loves them much more than he loves ordinary people. I thought this was very strange.

"You mean like the Bellevues?" I asked.

We had many troubled neighbors in our middle-class Boston neighborhood, but no one suffered as much as the Bellevue family. Mr. Bellevue was totally disabled and permanently confined to his bedroom. Mrs. Bellevue was grossly overweight and had advanced breast cancer. They had nine or ten children of all ages and races. Each had a different problem. They were retarded, unable to walk, had an unusual abnormality like a misshapen head or foot, jerky, uncontrollable motions, or could not speak. Because I knew nothing about foster children, I focused my fascination on why they were all so much thinner than their mother.

The Bellevues lived in a large, deteriorating home with a sagging, wraparound porch and a lawn that was never cut.

"Yes," my mother said. "God loves them very, very much."

"I'm glad God doesn't love us as much as them," I said out loud.

I had no real concept of God as a child. He was a loving, invisible power who lived in a church about a mile down the street. We went to visit Him every Sunday and said a prayer to him every night before bed. I never asked God for very much. When your life proceeds in a positive way, you feel in control of meeting your needs, and you remain healthy, you are likely to ask very little from God, and you receive little. At least you receive very little that you are confident comes from God. We were a God-fearing family, but we lived in a totally conscious, rational world. I knew nothing about instincts or even the existence of the unconscious.

What I did not understand as a child or for most of my adult life was that the widespread belief among mankind in a God comes from an inherited instinct. This God image is resident inside our unaware, unconscious minds. There is no God or morality within man without the help of his unconscious. Our spiritual unconscious is the place where we connect with our God.

Because the Bellevue family believed in God and, according to my mother, asked for His help every day, they always experienced God as positively present in their lives. God was their constant source of emotional support and comfort in their chaotic and uncontrollable world. In that sense, my mother was technically correct. God did love them more.

This book, however, is not about God or religion. We all have our own beliefs and a culturally and consciously unique image of our creator. It is about your relationship with your beneficial core and how it is always present to guide you and help you make the best decisions.

What is not widely known is that, besides having a God image—the instinctual urge toward God within our unconscious—you also have an inner voice that is part of our core. I am not speaking of a metaphorical voice. I am referring to a real voice we occasionally hear in our dreams. Historically that inner voice has been called the voice of God, a guardian angel, the inner conscience, the wise old man or the soul. The name of the voice does not matter.

We normally hear an inner voice in our dreams only when our values are in dire conflict, a higher moral value is needed to make a difficult decision, or we are in extreme need of advice. There are, however, notable exceptions.

Chosen Ones

Historically there have always been highly superior or "chosen" individuals who have exceptional access to their inner core. We may call these people "spiritual leaders," but they are not necessarily spiritual or leaders. We recognize these people intuitively. They demonstrate a strange, warm, magnetic energy, quiet knowledge, and exceptionally deep understanding. They are fully independent, ethical, creative, influential, adaptable, and purposeful beings. Most interestingly, wherever they go, the environment around them automatically improves. We know they are living the lives they were born to live, and we are naturally drawn to them.

Your Living Core

We are all original, born with a unique core of inherited values, ideals, motivations, and aspirations. This permanent, living, inner core stays with us for our entire life, consistently reminding us who we are, how we should live, and why we are here. It is our best resource for hidden knowledge, reliable guidance, self understanding, and fulfilling our purpose in life.

Opening up will not make you into a Mahatma Gandhi, but it will bring to light your most important goals in life. I can say that with certainty because I have experienced it firsthand. Remember, you do not need to be in big trouble before opening up to your core. You do, however, need to perform serious introspective work in order to be successful.

Assuming you meet the qualifications for participation noted in this chapter and you follow the program in the recommended sequence, you will succeed in opening up and communicating with your core. You will maintain 100 percent control of the entire process, allowing you to maintain complete privacy. While I will provide the necessary tools and methods to succeed, you will be doing all the work and receiving all the benefits.

Your ability to communicate with your core will be of invaluable assistance to you after reading this book and completing the program. Regardless of how difficult or complicated your life becomes, your core will always be there to help you make the best decisions. Your core knows the answers to the questions you most want answered. This includes:

❖ What is my purpose in life?

❖ What is my unique human nature?

❖ How do I deal with my inner conflicts?

❖ How can I protect myself from my negative urges?

❖ How do I make the best decision?

❖ Is there a connection between the unrelated events in my life?

Once you have finished this book and completed all the exercises, you will want to share your experience with your family and friends. You can share the name of this book and any general benefits you received from it, but I want you to live with your hard earned rewards privately. Opening up is intensely personal experience. Sharing your innermost thoughts and conclusions, could leave you psychologically vulnerable to the poorly considered opinions of others. Every individual is unique and responsible for his/her own growth and conclusions pertaining to his/her particular life journey. The best way to communicate your new self-knowledge, is by your thoughtful actions. By completing the five exercises in this book, you will know yourself and your purpose in life so much better.

Working on Your Own

This book allows me to privately share all the skills and exercises you need without intruding on or participating in your private self-discovery. It is critical you become aware of your core and discover the essential individual being you are before making contact with it. .

One of the most important design features of this book is that you will be working entirely on your own. Working alone has its advantages. You get to work at your own pace, avoid sharing potentially embarrassing experiences, and save money on a mentor's professional fees. The exercises necessary to communicate with your core, however, are designed exclusively for mentally healthy individuals.

None of these exercises utilize trances, hypnotism, hallucinations, psychoanalysis, drugs, mysticism, or religious practices to achieve results. To minimize the risk of contact with your collective (inherited) unconscious, which will be explained in chapter 1, I do not use any direct or implied two-way communication methods to the unconscious such as "active imagination." You will be listening to your core by paying close attention to your present-day dreams. There is no New Age practice of listening to others' voices, meditation, Transcendental Meditation (TM), or even prayer required to achieve your objectives.

How Long Will It Take to "Open Up to My Core"?

Depending upon how busy you are, this entire program should take approximately two months to complete on a part-time basis. Besides the reading, there are five mandatory self-awareness exercises. They cannot be rushed. Do not even think of skipping one of these exercises. The program will not work without fully completing the exercises in order.

As long as you can find a comfortable, private place, almost everything in this program can be done wherever and whenever you have the time. You need no special training to contact your core, but the process does require thinking, which is hard work. It also requires rigorous self-examination and total honesty. I suggest not starting the process until you are fully committed to completing it without any long period of interruption.

This book includes detailed instructions on how to conduct your self-awareness exercises. There are also sample questionnaires you can copy to organize your work. Be sure to store your paperwork in a secure location away from prying eyes. If you decide to work by computer, I recommend storing your information on either an encrypted computer file or an encrypted read/write CD-W. This way your private thoughts will always remain private. In chapter 2 you will learn exactly how to get organized and manage your program both securely and efficiently.

While I realize some readers may be familiar with one or more aspects of their inner core, you cannot skip any part of this program and hope to succeed. The reading and self-awareness projects serve three purposes: to prepare you for contact with your core, to advance your knowledge of the unconscious, and to engage in a long-term, cooperative, and respectful dialogue with your core. All three are necessary to make contact. Completing the entire program as written is critical. Always remember you will never study anything or communicate with anyone that knows you as completely as your core. There are no shortcuts to your success.

"Opening Up" Is Not for Everyone

Opening up is not recommended for everyone. The process was written for competent, mentally healthy, law-abiding, social adults of at least average intelligence. It is not recommended for young, immature people or the impaired elderly. Due to a small but real potential for adverse psychiatric consequences, people with mental health problems or symptoms such as antisocial behavior, depression, post-traumatic stress, mania, undue anxiety, anorexia, paranoia, persecution tendencies, or schizophrenia need to obtain a doctor's permission before participating.

Also, anyone can have a latent mental health problem, so if you find yourself feeling emotionally uncomfortable or anxious with any part of this book, I don't want you to continue. There could be something going on that you aren't aware of. Simply stop all activity, and your concerns should go away. If they continue, I suggest contacting your physician.

While this is a how-to book, it does not provide any advice or techniques for the treatment of any mental or physical injury, disease, or illness. Illness, disease, and injury require treatment by a qualified, competent, licensed professional with specialized training in his or her field.

Preparing for contact with your core may seem a little strange at first. While the process may not be immediately appealing, please read on for a while before deciding to quit. Know that you will soon receive beneficial results. I still follow the same techniques I recommend to you because the process is fun, and I need all the help I can get for my own life.

Your Goals

I would like you to start by writing down your goals for reading this book and what you hope to learn from your core. While you can expect your goals and interests to change by the end of the book, having well-considered and frequently reviewed goals will make this experience more rewarding. If you are working on your computer, create a file called "Goals," and write down your expectations with today's date.

Chapter I:

A Beautiful, Blended Mind

The Conscious, Rational Mind

We all use our rational and aware conscious minds to see ourselves as individuals and make logical decisions. It is our rational thinking that drives us to constantly acquire new knowledge and consciousness. We grow our consciousness and expand our reasoning through ongoing education. While we search for knowledge all our lives, only understanding can satisfy us.

Being aware is how we understand and navigate our world, but if we only had rational, conscious minds, we would be markedly different from who we are now. The rational mind is individualistic and selfish. It is clinical in all our actions. There would be logical rules for everything in our lives, we would be stubborn to a fault, and unwilling to ever make an exception. Our world would be based entirely on personal observation and statistics. Nothing would be accepted as unknowable. We would control everything we experience, and our words would become as real as physical objects. Man would become his own God.

The Unaware, Unconscious Mind

In the famous book *The Interpretation of Dreams*, published in 1900, Sigmund Freud was the first to theorize about the existence of the unconscious mind. For more than four thousand years prior, educated individuals, religious experimenters, mystics, and adventurers experimented with their mysterious inner worlds by going into trances, which were usually aided by psychedelic drugs. Their goals were familiar: to promote dreams, heal, solve problems, overcome pain and fear, increase strength, and most importantly communicate with God. The term trance today has been discredited in favor of the more scientific term "hypnosis."

Most contemporary scientists since Charles Darwin agree that the human mind has evolved from a much more primitive mind. Biologically speaking, our human mind is millions of years old. Ancient man, unlike us, was not consciously an individual person. He was part of tribal group that shared a common essence or soul. He was not in control of his world and did not even think he was a member of the superior species. Because the cause of all events was external to his understanding, ancient man was preoccupied with magic and his God(s). He was as moral as we are today, but given his primitive existence, he had different ideals and values.

In real life we are always thinking with both our aware and unaware minds. The idea of two separate minds inside one brain doesn't seem very logical to us today, especially when we can't see our unconscious mind on an MRI. The best objective evidence of unconscious activity is an observable unsolved mystery. Based upon fMRI (functional MRI) research, unconscious energy is believed to materialize in our observable brains out of nothingness, only to disappear again in nanoseconds. This unconscious energy does not appear to reside in any one special place. I think it helps to visualize the unconscious as the archaic and unaware brain functions we all have.

In his 2010 "Comprehensive Survey of Contemporary Research of the Unconscious", published by the *Advances in Cognitive Psychology*, Louis Augusto distinguished unconscious knowledge from conscious knowledge as independent of conscious thought, age, and IQ, more robust, holistic, and inflexible, and more task performance-based than conceptual. Unconscious information is described as having a different quality than conscious knowledge, and it is speculated to come from a different visual pathway. The unconscious has long been observed making wellness decisions entirely without the support of the conscious mind.

We cannot explain how we acquire unconscious knowledge or how we access it. We cannot even verbalize how the information is organized. We receive more information through our unconscious than we can experience through our conscious, and we process this information much faster. Researchers at Columbia University Medical Center found that test images that appear and disappear so quickly they escape conscious awareness still produce unconscious activity in the brain. This can be detected with the latest fMRI neuroimaging machines. The conscious mind is hundreds of milliseconds slower than our unconscious processes.

A Second Visual Stream

Current interest in the unconscious has been increasing due in part due to the research of A. D. Milner, and M. A. Goodale. They have proposed that "we have two separate but interacting visual systems that have evolved for the perception of objects and the control of actions directed at those objects." The theory suggests we all may have a second visual stream for visual stimuli.

This theory of two visual pathways "corresponds to the segregation between conscious and unconscious processing of visual stimuli." While still an unproven theory, there are many areas of cognitive research that support it, including "blindsight." Blindsight is a phenomenon in which patients with damage in their primary visual cortex can still tell where an object is, although they claim they cannot see it. In other words, research has shown that blind subjects can sense an object's location, grasp for it correctly, and even navigate objects in its path. This second visual path has also been associated with higher levels of understanding, including facial expressions, and emotions. Research studies even suggest some subjects may be covertly forming beliefs and intentions they are unaware of in behavioral terms. Anecdotally, while the conscious mind is quieted by applying general anesthesia, many of the functions of the unconscious have been observed to remain totally unaffected.

Our unconscious is uncharted and filled with sparks and bits of energy that cluster, connect, and vanish instantaneously. Within our unconscious there is no concept of time or spatial limitations. C. G. Jung said the unconscious contains "all your intentions and your urges, everything you know but you are not thinking about, everything you forgot, everything you saw but did not notice or choose to remember, and even the next random thought you are going to have." While the unconscious mind is a biological partner to the conscious mind, to remain psychologically healthy, the conscious mind must always remain in control of the whole mind.

Freud's Topography of the Mind

In his paper on the unconscious, Freud published a topographical visualization of the human mind. It shows our functioning brain can be divided into three systems: the conscious, preconscious, and unconscious. This same Freudian topography is still in limited use today, primarily in Europe.

This modified iceberg model demonstrates Freud's theory that the human conscious is only a small part of what we are (10 percent). To Freud, the conscious mind contained everything we are aware of. His preconscious mind contained information we were not actively aware of but could consciously access if needed. This includes information we are capable of recollecting with effort such as the names of past teachers and childhood friends. The Freudian unconscious contained all of our base emotions, feelings, impulses, and beliefs.

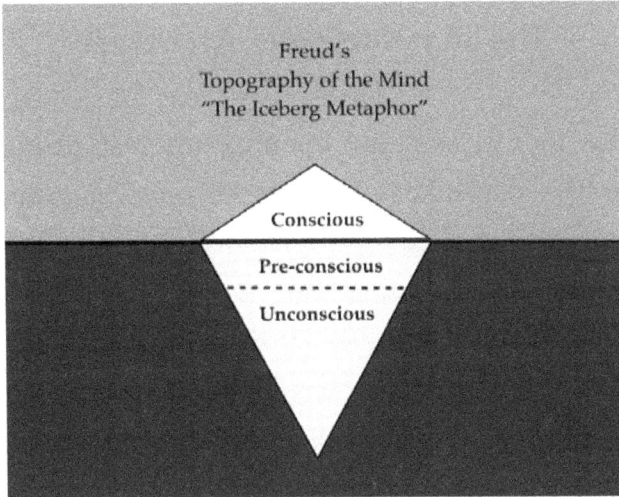

Freud's
Topography of the Mind
"The Iceberg Metaphor"

Conscious

Pre-conscious
- - - - - - - - - - - - - -
Unconscious

Freud's topography is especially interesting to me because of the preconscious. The preconscious area represents a place where some unconscious material is stored for easy access by the conscious as needed. The preconscious mind suggests not all human mental activity is either conscious or unconscious.

We intuitively recognize that we live in a blended state of aware and unaware consciousness quite frequently. Whether we are daydreaming, driving for long distances on the interstate, watching TV, listening to music, reading a book, or recovering from the flu with a high fever, we know we are not 100 percent conscious. Some philosophers have long suggested we live our entire lives in a state of reduced or altered consciousness.

The Superior "God" Archetype

The foundations for opening up rest primarily upon the psychological research of C. G. Jung, a prominent Swiss psychiatrist and former student of Sigmund Freud. Jung, the noted researcher on dreams, theorized there are two separate parts to Freud's unconscious: a personal unconscious, containing all the individual experiences unique to each of us, and a primitive collective unconscious, containing the blueprints of all the images and instincts necessary for us to inherit the universal nature of man as a species. He theorized that everything within our collective unconscious was represented and triggered by an unconscious image such as a God image. He called these archaic, imprinted images archetypes. He suggested we receive them biologically, perhaps even through our DNA. Today we speculate whether Jung's collective unconscious may inherited by epigenetics, also known as non DNA cell memory traits.

While Jung and Freud both agreed the strongest instinct in man was procreation, the second most powerful, according to Jung, was the God image. Jung estimated there were thousands of archetypes contained within each human being. Some other examples of Jungian archetypes include "the ruler who takes control," "the hero who saves the day," and "the outlaw who breaks the rules."

Jung found the God image was the only archetype (instinct) capable of commanding control over all the other archetypes, including man's sex drive. The God archetype has been and still appears to be completely autonomous. It always appears without warning, surfacing anywhere in the world with awesome and fearsome effect. Under the power of the God instinct, soldiers can be blinded, the weather manipulated, and the weak supported to conquer the mighty.

The God image is as universally evident today as ever, changing world politics, spawning revolutions and terrorism, and even helping millions of men and women control their addictions through Alcoholics Anonymous. Jung espoused the notion that our unconscious God archetype is the existential human source of all human morality, and by our conscious awareness and agreement with certain values, man created ethics.

The Emotional Unconscious

If you experience the sudden desire to do or obtain something, it is very easy to determine the source of that idea. Our rational, conscious mind is not emotional. When we make a rational, conscious decision based upon objective criteria alone, we are not even aware of our feelings.

Our unconscious desires and instincts, however, are always emotional. The unconscious influences the rational mind by releasing archetypal images. These automatically trigger the emotional urge or instinct designed to produce a specific action. A sudden, unwanted romantic attraction to someone is a common example of a procreation urge from the collective unconscious. The greater the emotional attachment to the archetype, the harder it is to consciously control the urge. One reason why we study our unconscious is to learn how we can manage our negative instincts.

Most of us erroneously think we are 95 percent conscious and only 5 percent unconscious. As a result, we never pay attention to our unconscious. Because we believe our rational, conscious mind is in control 95 percent of the time, we are certain we make fair and ethical decisions 95 percent of the time. We see ourselves as good, decent, honest people living in a rational world, despite overwhelming evidence there is chaos and evil all around us. What you will discover by opening up to your core is a far more powerful and ever-present unconscious world than you ever imagined.

There is a disagreement among scientists about why we need an unconscious. The most popular and intuitively correct theories suggest a combination of two reasons. On one hand, the unconscious acts like a computer recycle bin for unwanted or unneeded information. On the other hand, it is known to support our conscious mind with enhanced knowledge and valuable inherited information.

The Unconscious as a Recycle Bin

Our unconscious mind does function as a recycle bin. This is where we place all the things we don't want to be aware of, including bad memories, buried feelings, overlooked hypocrisies, ugly thoughts, and all our hidden, selfish motivations. It also includes our darkest, most hidden desires, our depravities, the things we fear the most, our repressed aspirations, and even our unexpressed ideals.

For many of us, we live with a recycle bin full of things we wish we could dispose of. Unfortunately it takes a lot of mental energy to save all this information in our recycle bin. Jung suggests that simply becoming conscious of hidden, unconscious material releases energy that can be used for other activities or held in reserve.

The Mind Is a Closed System

Jung frequently described the mind as a relatively "closed system." What that means is that, at any given time, we each have a relatively limited amount of energy available for all our conscious and unconscious mental activities. While the brain is consistently replenished biologically with new energy, within the time of a single event, the mind is operating on a fixed energy budget. No matter what our needs, the brain can only spend as much energy as it has available. When one part of the brain needs energy to perform work, it must take the energy away from another mental function or access excess energy from its reserve.

For example, we're driving to an appointment, and a truck pulls out in front of us. No matter what we were thinking about a moment before, all our attention is now focused on the new problem: how to avoid an accident. Only later will we be capable of going back to the thoughts we were having prior to the incident. We don't do this reallocation of energy consciously. It takes place automatically based upon our immediate needs.

Jung's opinion of the brain is consistent with the famous nineteenth century law of conservation of energy (the first law of thermodynamics). In isolated, closed systems, the total amount of energy remains constant over time. This suggests the total energy can neither be created nor destroyed. Therefore it has to be transformed from one form to another or transferred from one place to another. It stands to reason that the more mental energy we have in reserve for a crisis, the better we will perform.

Besides acting as a recycle bin, Jung also saw the unconscious acting in promotion and support of the rational conscious, primarily through our dreams. Dreams provide additional information to the conscious mind every night. He also believed dream content helps us discover and resolve emotional problems. Recurring dreams, Jung thought, was proof that our unconscious was demanding the attention of the conscious. Both our personal unconscious and collective unconscious regularly produce full-feature metaphorical dreams.

Psychoanalysis

Jung proposed the process of "individuation" was necessary for a healthy person to become whole. By use of psychoanalysis and dream analysis, Jung's subjects worked to eliminate internal conflicts and integrate the negative content of the unconscious with the conscious. A primary benefit of individuation was releasing energy that then became available in reserve for other mental activities.

The process worked, in theory, because it creates a cooperative balance between the conscious and the unconscious. Today, psychoanalysis is considered a highly specialized but nonscientific mental health treatment. It is considered to be highly effective but expensive and very time-consuming.

Opening up is designed only for those who are mentally healthy and does not require the assistance of a psychoanalyst. While you will be logging your dreams, you will review only the dreams of your personal unconscious. Then you will obtain well-defined, beneficial knowledge received from your core. (Unlike psychoanalysis, you will never review any of the powerful and negative fantasy dreams that sometimes emerge from your primitive, archaic collective unconscious.) With this program, there will be no in-depth dream analysis like that performed in psychoanalysis.

Having Mental Energy in Reserve

We all know from experience that being in poor health or under great stress can reduce our ability to think normally. When you are sick or tired, it's easy to fall behind in life and ignore the smaller problems. It is even natural in times of great distress to feel less empathy toward others. I have read that soldiers who have to sleep out in the open for long periods of time become more aggressive and temporarily lose their capacity for empathy. This would not be a conscious decision on the soldier's part. It's an unconscious response to the reallocation of mental energy, and it is necessary due to their extreme environment.

Unfortunately, it is just when we need our problem-solving skills the most that we may find the least amount of reserve energy available. As part of "opening up," you will be looking at simple ways to increase your reserve mental energy and improve your ability to make the best decisions in times of stress. You will start this process by carefully observing and investigating yourself. What you will find is you are a unique, beautiful blend of consciousness and unconsciousness, fortified by unique values and ideals. You already have everything you need to achieve your purpose in life and speak with your core.

Chapter 2
Getting Organized

The Commitment

If you woke up this morning and decided you wanted to run a half marathon, it would take you, on average, six months to complete a conservative, step-by-step physical training program. It should take you only about two months to complete this opening up training program. While it took me years of trial and error to design this program, it should take you less than an hour a day to manage the program, not counting the five special self-awareness projects.

Preparing to receive guidance from your core is disarmingly simple and accessible. It is, however, mentally challenging and thought provoking if done correctly. You will soon be asked to be critically honest and objective in getting to know yourself. For some of you, the five awareness exercises will be extremely difficult. The secret to your future success is to take as much time as you need to do each exercise correctly.

"The core program" does require a consistency of effort. The completion of this program is in many ways analogous to the process of making a new friend. The more time you spend with a friend doing things you are both interested in, the faster you will bond. The same is true of your relationship with your core.

That is why I do not recommend taking any lengthy breaks from your work once you start. Think about what happens when you start to make a good friend but then don't see him/her for a long time. If you take too long of a break, you may have to start over to rekindle the relationship. Similarly you cannot rush the process. If you don't have the time now, I suggest putting the program off until you do. Remember the first law of Khufu, the pharaoh of Egypt for whom the Great Pyramid of Giza was built: Nothing is ever built on time or within a budget. If you are patient and follow the other suggestions of this book, I know you will succeed.

Your Core Is Your Best Friend

Learning about your core is a unique educational experience. What makes it so unusual is that your inner core knows everything about you, but you know almost nothing about it. While there is only one you, your first self-awareness exercise will introduce you to the many different psychic entities that appear as a part of you in your dreams. You will observe how they seem to operate independently of your conscious thoughts while trying to influence your conscious mind. This in itself is a startling discovery.

You will see things inside of you you never knew existed. You will uncover secrets you have kept from yourself, including your highest ideals and aspirations. There may be some things you are not proud of, but you deserve sympathetic love and attention. As long as you maintain a tolerant attitude about the truth you discover, you will be empowered and exhilarated.

Your core is both a part of you and your soon-to-be-discovered best friend. Don't we all have a best friend we don't always agree with, who sometimes wants to do things we don't like, who tells us the truth when we don't want to hear it, or who seems to be in one complicated situation after another? Friends sometimes understand us better than we do. They help us understand what is important, and they love us despite all our faults. To maintain our successful relationship, we must learn how to disagree without hurting each other. Despite all their faults, we still love them because of their overall goodness and how we feel when we are with them. We do not merely want them in our lives; we need them in our lives. Yes, our positive core is very much like a good friend.

I suggest going slowly with this program. Pay attention to everything you learn, and decide in advance not to make any self-judgments. Don't forget that by reading this book and becoming more self-aware, you have not changed. You have been living with yourself all your life. Knowledge may change your understanding of who you are, but it will not change who you are.

Important Considerations

Our best intentions in this program are important. They support our effort to forge a positive relationship with our core. While it is possible to use our core for hostile or immoral intentions, you will experience serious psychological problems if you do. Think about devil worshiping as an example. Willingly associating with the negative urges of the collective unconscious has long been known to produce serious psychological damage.

Please also keep in mind that having access to your core will not make you wealthy, treat an illness, or fix your relationship problems. It will not improve your social life, make you more religious, or help you find out exactly what went wrong in your past. With the help of your core, however, you can discover the meaning of your life, gain knowledge well beyond your conscious abilities, and create a new harmony with your inner self.

Selecting Your Work Location

There are two separate types of activities requiring your organization: dream logging and self-awareness projects. Dream logging especially has many important location-related requirements. If you do not live alone, making the time and finding a place to do your dream logging will require some thought and planning.

As part of the program, you will be writing down or recording your dreams as soon as you wake up, either during the middle of the night or first thing in the morning. Recording your dreams while still sitting in bed is the gold standard. You are still half asleep, but you will be relaxed and free from any thoughts other than your dream. This is the best time and place to narrate your dreams. If you sleep alone, the biggest problem will be fighting falling back asleep. If you sleep with someone else, however, privacy and consideration will require you to record your dreams somewhere else.

While it is not mandatory, I highly suggest you record all your dreams with a digital recorder. If you will be disturbing someone by your dictation, you can always take the recorder into the bathroom or another room to do a quick narration. Remember, time is of the essence. It is critically important you record your dream as soon as you awaken. Within a few minutes, you will forget valuable details of your dream.

My first choice was to stumble into my bathroom to narrate a dream. Over time I realized this was not an attractive option. First of all, unless you have a fancy toilet seat, you will not be very comfortable. If you sit there too long, your legs will get numb. You can overcome this if you are lucky enough to have a big bathroom and can install a comfortable chair.

You also need to test the acoustics of the bathroom, especially if it is 100 percent tiled. You don't want to be overheard by family members or, even worse, a next-door neighbor as you narrate a private dream. There is also the matter of your house protocols. In my home, going to the bathroom means I am up and available for a distracting conversation with my wife, who is a light sleeper. Sometimes a more distant room is best.

After a trial bathroom period, I moved my dream dictation work into my home office. My wife is used to giving me privacy there, and I have a terrific orthopedic chair. The biggest disadvantage of using my home office is that I wake up faster there. As a result I have to narrate my dreams more quickly. There is something about being in a work environment that gets your mind working faster. There are also more distractions in your home office than the bathroom. You need to be focused. The goal is to narrate the dream as quickly as possible and get back to sleep or start your day.

Strategically you may decide it is best to initially handwrite your dreams by your bedside, assuming you have some light. This is not as successful as immediate narration, but it may be required if you don't have the private space you need. If you choose this method, you need to review the dream details as soon as possible.

Self-awareness projects require a longer investment of time and energy per session. There are five special projects used in this program. Each project has a writing phase and a separate evaluation phase. Special projects do not require a daily time commitment. They are better tackled over a weekend or when you have a free evening.

Use a Digital Recorder

I highly recommend using a digital recorder with speech recognition software to record your dreams quickly. Then automatically convert your speech into readable text on your computer. Some dictation software, such as Dragon Naturally Speaking, allows you to use a handheld digital voice recorder or even your iPhone or iPod. While it is possible to complete the "core program" by manually typing everything on your keyboard or, if you don't have a computer, keeping all your work in handwritten form, these tedious methods will detract from your enjoyment of the program. I do not recommend them if you can avoid them.

Every day you will be plugging your digital recorder into your computer to convert your dream recording(s) into a text file, or you will be writing down your dream on a large pad of paper. This should take an average of twenty to thirty minutes a day, once you become proficient.

If you do decide to buy a digital recorder, learn how to use it before you start the program. They take a little time to get used to. I don't want you to forget your first dream because you can't figure out how the buttons work or there are no batteries are in the house. Also make sure all accessory cables and plugs are installed properly. Make sure everything works like it should.

You Come First

I suggest you start planning your dream logging work by acknowledging something. While everyone else in your life is very important, in this program, you are the most important person. The commitment to yourself first is absolutely necessary. We are each given only one life to live. There is no one more important to your life than you. You need to make the time necessary for yourself.

Your first decision is when you're going to do your work. Remember, this is a private, personal program you will not be sharing with anyone. Having a wide-open schedule is rare these days. For most of us, the best time is going to be either early in the morning or later in the evening. If that does not work for you, the best answer may be fitting the time between regularly scheduled activities. The regularity of the other activities will help keep you on schedule.

Not When You First Arrive Home from Work

Coming home from work and immediately doing your self-awareness work can be difficult. If you are still stressed from your workday, or you have a spouse and children who need your attention, try your best to make alternative plans. If you foresee having a conflict or being subject to uncomfortable family questions, it's better to address that problem before it starts. Careful scheduling and finding ways to compensate others for their loss of time with you will usually do the trick.

If you are accustomed to having cocktails when you come home from work, this is not the right time to work on your program. Alcohol is a depressant and will negatively affect your ability to remember, narrate, and evaluate yourself. If you are currently drinking heavily on a regular basis, you need to either cut back to no more than two drinks a day or put off your participation in this program.

Handling Your Family and Friends

Despite your best efforts, those close to you will be interested in what you are doing. I do not recommend you disclose any details of the program or what you are doing. My advice is to honestly and factually answer their questions but in a limited way. Simple answers should help such as: I am very interested in my dreams, I am trying to remember a dream, I like to write down my thoughts, this relaxes me, I am trying to remember something, or I am working on a project.

Your attitude and demeanor is very important while doing this project. You can be sure your family will become alarmed if you markedly change your behavior, for better or worse, during the program. In an extreme case, it may be necessary for you to exercise total concealment in order to participate. Whatever you decide, avoid sharing any aspect of your work with anyone. Never do any work on anyone else's computer, and never write anything project-related on your work computer. While you are using your employer's computer, software could be recording your work.

If you are a person who hates working on a computer screen, you may want to print your work frequently to review it. Any printer (bubble jet, black and white laser, or color printer) will work just fine. If you are going to print your work, however, please be sure to buy a cheap paper shredder to dispose of your unsaved work immediately after you are done. Don't forget, you always need a good surge protector between the computer and the power source to protect your work in the event of a power failure.

Have you thought about how you want to apply your new mental energy? One suggestion is to develop a personal skill that is currently underdeveloped. It is time to once again review and rethink your goals for this program. What specific information would you like to ask of your core?

Chapter 3
About Dreams

Dreaming

Dreaming is said to be a universal human attribute. While science is unable to prove why we dream, we do know that dreaming helps keep us psychologically healthy. Our dreams originate in our unconscious and provide a conduit for our unconscious to communicate with our conscious mind. If you were to do nothing more than record your dreams and reread them later, it would have a profoundly positive effect on your conscious thinking.

REM (rapid eye movement) sleep research confirms we dream, on average, two hours a night. It is mostly five to ten minute dreams early in the night and fifteen to twenty minute dreams near daybreak. Dreams use symbolic images to create a message for the conscious mind in a story format. Unfortunately, because we each interpret symbols differently based upon culture and experiences, we all use a different dream language. That is why there is no best-selling book on dream symbols and their meanings.

The dream world is obviously very different from the rational world. Within the same dream, we can be old, young, or both. We can be here, there, or anywhere, including nowhere. In a second, we can change everything we cannot alter in reality: time, place, character circumstances, and quality of everything we see. For the mobility-handicapped and the incarcerated, dreams are a substitute for freedom.

Our dream actions are exaggerated, compact in meaning, and usually very edgy. We can be performing a superhuman feat or participating in a primitive, heinous act. If the phone rings, we seamlessly incorporate the sound into our dream. Remarkably, when we dream, we truly live every experience and feel every emotion as authentically as if it were real. While it is nearly impossible to interpret our dreams, we can easily obtain valuable information from them, if we learn to pay attention.

Numinous Dreams

According to Jung, we have three basic categories of dreams: numinous (God) dreams, collective (archaic) dreams, and personal dreams. The word numinous comes from the Latin cult word *numen*, which means a guardian, spirit, or godhead. Without any exaggeration, if you have a numinous dream, you will *know* God is communicating with you personally. It is commonly believed that only a few people with pure spiritual intentions will ever experience a numinous dream. While numinous dreams are extremely rare, you may be fortunate enough to have one while participating in this program.

You can always identify a numinous dream by the unique dream place, your emotions, and the unusual aftereffects. These dreams are visions rather than action stories. They take place in intuitively sacred locations, which are not created by or for human beings. The landscape of the dream appears infinite, and time is everlasting. We know this place does not ever decay or change. If we wanted to enter this place, we would have to leave our world behind. All at once, we could understand the incomprehensible. We would feel two powerful emotions simultaneously: a trembling fear and an awesome fascination.

You cannot figure out how you understand this vision, but it fills you with superior knowledge and understanding. The dream is totally unexpected and restores your faith in God. You may feel possessed by the unity, beauty, and ecstasy of God's perfection. Many of these dreams contain moving lights described as sparks, stars, a perfect light, a cleansing or destructive fire, or mystical auras. Other elements include exotic smells, tastes, colors, and sounds. The vision will also contain a prophecy that fills you with hope.

Numinous dreams range from extremely valuable to life-changing. As previously mentioned, there is rarely an accompanying voice of God. While under the irresistible control of this enormously powerful dream, your emotions may crystallize with your thoughts and convictions to compel you to improve your behavior.

You usually remember these dreams for years, but the details will begin to fade after a week or two. If you ever have such a dream, record it in as much detail as possible for your long-term personal benefit.

Collective Dreams

Collective dreams from the collective unconscious are dramatically different. They are inherently archaic and have an emotional fairy-tale quality. They contain unfamiliar, bizarre characters such as fearsome, ancient warriors, classical maidens in distress, and mythical beasts. Archaic dreams are the dreams we most frequently associate with nightmares due to their raw, primitive, and incomprehensible content.

You will not be familiar with collective dream characters, and the messages can be violent and morally disturbing. Other collective dream themes include the insatiable desire for all forms of pleasure, the devil incarnate, the compulsive need for total control, and comic book-style heroic behavior. These dreams are often so repulsive you won't even want to read them. Interpreting collective dreams can be injurious to your health.

These archaic dreams are especially dangerous because they can draw us into a state of elevated emotion. It is human to be drawn into emotions by simply observing them. We laugh at jokes we do not understand, cry watching sad movies, and even get swept up at political rallies. If you start to believe there is something wrong with you, these negative fantasies could amplify your emotions and create fear. Don't be concerned. There is nothing wrong with you. These dreams are about all of mankind's biological history and are not about you personally. They have no power over you.

While the collective unconscious is not intrinsically evil, its instincts and emotions can lead us to make evil choices. The powerful dream images produced by the collective unconscious frequently behave as a ferocious collection of demon urges. The same is true for artificially induced dreams, used to gain knowledge about the unconscious mind for personal gain. Some of the evil we see in the world is the direct result of unscrupulous individuals deliberately connecting with their collective unconscious for immoral purposes.

Always be wary of a highly emotional dream. It could be a collective dream masquerading as a personal dream. If you are dreaming about your strong desire for money, prestige, power, romantic passion, or associating with famous people, you may be in the grip of your collective unconscious.

If an otherwise present-day, personal dream contains any collective archaic element such as a magical object, mythical creatures, or fairytale characters, then it is not a personal dream but a collective dream. Sometimes a collective dream can look like a personal dream. Be on the lookout.

It is perfectly normal to experience a nightmare once or possibly twice a year. If you notice, however, you are starting to experience this type of distressing dream more frequently, you should put your program on hold and seek medical advice before proceeding. Nightmares could lead you to sleep disorders or be indicative of a more serious problem.

Personal Dreams

Personal, present-day dreams are the most common type of dream. They originate in the personal unconscious and are the only type of dream you will review as part of this program. The dream takes place in current time with characters wearing everyday day clothing.

Without special training, we cannot hope to understand every aspect of our personal dreams. The truth is, not everything in personal dreams is so important that it needs to be understood. Without any special attention, almost all your past personal dreams have gone unnoticed. Yet they resolved themselves over time. Some scientists even theorize that the conscious mind completely understands all unconscious dreams, and as a result, there is no reason for us to pay any attention to them at all. So the question is, why would you want to pay attention to your personal dreams?

Why We Review Personal Dreams

Dreams are one of the only ways our core can communicate important, time-sensitive information to the conscious mind. If we wish to communicate with our core, dreams are the only reliable and natural way to make that happen. This is not a new idea. A quick review of literature reveals that dreams have been the preferred method of spiritual enlightenment from God and the human soul for more than five thousand years.

Not everything in our personal dreams, however, is useful or understandable. My experience is that only about half of personal dreams contain specific information that can be helpful in day-to-day life. Within dreams there are two reliable, positive benefits: awareness and prophecy. Awareness lets us know there is something wrong with our conscious attitudes and behavior. Prophecy dreams tell us we are traveling in the wrong direction, or they point out the right direction for us to go. Awareness and prophecies contained in personal dreams are the only dream information we are after. There is no other information contained in your personal dreams that will be consistently beneficial to you. Because of the frightening and inappropriate images contained in collective dreams, you will continue to ignore them as you have all your life.

One way we can quickly understand our dreams is to focus on our dream characters. They each play a separate role such as a father, mother, or priest. Each represents a separate ideal or emotion, and they never play more than one part in a dream. Our unconscious contains thousands of instinctual images. In our dreams, each dream character is actually a part of us. Just as we all have multiple real-life roles, we are represented in dreams as a collection of separate instincts, each operating as a separate avatar. Our dreams are almost exclusively about us. Outside people rarely visit us in our dreams.

Personal Dreams Happen in Real-Life Places

Our personal dreams take place on a symbolic stage representing a familiar, real-life place. Personal dreams are usually about a current, important situation you are dealing with. On this dream stage, your unconscious instincts get to perform with each other in order to show your conscious something it does not know about the real-life situation.

Dream Characters Are Emotions

If, during your dream, you see an angry character, you should understand that a part of you is angry. This can be valuable information if you were unaware of your true feelings about that particular situation.

Regardless of who these characters look like, it is always their behavior and emotion that define them.

Your unconscious uses your emotions to get the attention of your conscious mind. A dream that has no emotion attached to it is always less important than one containing emotion. The more emotional the dream, the more important it is to your unconscious. Recurring dreams are considered especially important because the unconscious values the message so much it keeps repeating it. All the sensations we experience consciously coexist inside our dreams. The most intense characters are always the most important ones to examine.

Your dreams are much easier to understand if you know what life situation is being reenacted. Your one big clue is that the majority of dreams are about things we have been doing over the past day or two. If you want to understand what is going on in a dream, name all the characters by their emotions or behavior, and describe what they did to each other.

As the first exercise of your opening up program, you will log your personal dreams and learn how to obtain only helpful information from them. Incidentally, do not ever think a dream is telling you that you are terrific and deserve a big reward. Dreams from the core never flatter us. They always want to improve us and make us more personally responsible for our actions.

Avoid In-Depth Dream Analysis

Because it is nearly impossible to understand everything in our dreams, there is a significant possibility of misinterpreting them. When you start believing in something you only imagine is true, you can get into trouble very quickly. As a result, you need to use a focused approach to review your dreams for helpful information. By avoiding the negative unconscious, you can remain grounded in the positive. Please do not get sidetracked by psychological dream analysis. Besides being potentially dangerous, dream analysis will ruin your chances of success in contacting your core.

Why You Used to Forget Your Dreams

You have probably wondered why you forget your dreams. It's because the brain chemicals necessary to create a long-term memory are suppressed during REM sleep. In this exercise, despite the difficulties, you will try to remember as many of your dreams as possible. I am going to teach you a trick, though, to dramatically improve your dream memory.

By using a simple bedtime suggestion, your unconscious will get the message you want to remember your dreams, and it will help you do that. Over time, your dreams will become more vivid and easier to understand. Do not be surprised if you have more than a hundred dreams to review later in the program. I know you will be especially fascinated to learn what your core has been telling you every night.

Prophecy Dreams Are Not Divinely Inspired

Personal dreams frequently come with some element of prophecy. Please do not misconstrue the word *prophecy* as meaning your dreams are divinely inspired. They are not. A prophecy dream is either a warning from your unconscious core that something negative will happen if things remain the same, or it is a foreshadowing that something positive will happen if you work to support it.

In truth, your core has no knowledge of your future decisions. You alone are in control of your future choices. As for your future, your core is just as interested in what will happen as you. Your future is entirely speculative for your core. What frequently happens, however, is your core warns you about something that likely will happen in the future. This is based upon the core's superior knowledge of your past and present. Prophecy dreams are extremely useful tools to help us rethink our specific decisions and actions, but like everything in life, you cannot accept them as infallible.

Your core has a complete picture of your life and growth potential. It also knows the ideal blueprint for your future. By paying attention to your beneficial dreams, you will learn to trust and rely upon your core's fundamental wisdom as a supplement to your conscious understanding of your real-life experiences. By paying close attention to your core's communications over time, you will more easily understand the messages and be able to make the best decisions. You should always look to your core as an excellent resource for information not otherwise available. Like all resources, however, you must learn to pay close attention to certain key details and take full responsibility for using that information.

Your Conscience Has an Agenda

Keep in mind our conscience has their own agenda. Your intended purpose in life is the goal of your core, regardless of what you consciously want to do. We must always investigate the advice given by our core to ensure we are doing what we really want and that it is good for us.

Your unconscious is just like your physical body. It has functional strengths and weaknesses. We all have unique life histories and cultures. Some of us are more corrupted and conflicted in our unconscious thinking than others. Prior actions can even do damage to the core. That is why your conscious mind must remain in charge of everything you do. Communicating with your core will help you make better decisions, but it will not make decisions for you.

While your dreams help you grow, learn, and make better decisions, they will also make you aware of your internal conflicts. All our hidden ideals and desires are capable of becoming emotional dream characters. These pure energy characters have a different quality and intensity. They can conflict with your rational decisions and even urge you to do things not in your best interest. Sometimes they even go to war with each other.

Don't Be Afraid of Your Unconscious

Some people are afraid of their unconscious. They see evil all around them, and they believe it exists within them as well. They may have seen the horrors of mental illness in a family member or been exposed to the perversions of mass hysteria in a primitive society. Our unconscious does contain primitive, negative instincts that once were necessary to survive but are no longer appropriate for modern living. We don't know what to do if a pride of lions were to suddenly hunt us down while we were barbequing in the park, but our unconscious does. When we suddenly become aware of these ancient and sometimes violent instincts, we naturally become frightened. Our archaic, primitive instincts are not usually gentle.

The most serious mental health problems come from biological problems that disconnect the conscious mind from the unconscious mind. Researchers have found evidence that the unconscious mind of schizophrenics is usually working properly. The problem is the conscious mind is not receiving the unconscious mind's signals properly. Mentally healthy people do not need to fear the disease of insanity. If you choose to give your unconscious total control over your life, however, you will experience mental health problems. While the collective unconscious is not inherently evil, it can corrupt your thinking and lead you to do evil things. Never use your unconscious for negative purposes.

Chapter 4
Your Sweet Personal Dreams

How to Remember Your Personal Dreams

It is not enough to simply decide you want to record your dreams. You need to let your unconscious know you want to start remembering all your dreams. Every present-day dream you remember might contain important, beneficial information.

To ask for the assistance of your unconscious, you need to perform a simple, nightly bedtime suggestion right before you fall asleep (see below). Without your nightly suggestion, your dream memory will drop precipitously in only a few days. Repeating the same suggestion nightly throughout the program will ensure a consistent volume of dreams and greatly support your preparation process.

After you are comfortable in bed and finished with your final thoughts and intentions, make the following silent suggestion to your unconscious self. While you perform this suggestion, think about remembering your dreams and how very interested you are in them.

Breathe in slowly, and hold your breath. Say only with your thoughts, "I want to remember my dreams." As you exhale slowly, say to yourself, "Ten." Breathe in, and hold your breath. Say again with your thoughts, "I want to remember my dreams." As you exhale slowly, say to yourself, "Nine." At this point, your unconscious is expecting you to repeat the same suggestion followed by the number eight. To get the attention and interest of your unconscious, you are going to repeat the suggestion but skip the number eight. Go instead to seven. Breathe in, and hold your breath. Say with your thoughts, "I want to remember my dreams." As you exhale slowly, say, "Seven." After the number seven, you should repeat the suggestion with numbers in the correct, descending sequence from six to zero. When done, repeat four more times. Try to complete all five of your repetition sets, but don't be concerned if you fall asleep before finishing. Your unconscious will receive the suggestion.

After only a few nights of suggestion, you will find your dream memories will increase in both detail and frequency. Many of you will ultimately experience full-featured dreams that include input from all five senses.

Watch What You Say

The exact words you say in your bedtime suggestion or, for that matter, in a prayer are very important because your unconscious takes your words literally. If you are used to saying a bedtime prayer, I strongly suggest you pay close attention to the exact words contained in the prayer.

I recently had a conversation with a hypnotherapist who works extensively with elderly nursing home residents. He relayed a common anxiety among his aging clients. The problem came from the popular prayer, "Now I Lay Me Down to Sleep." This classic eighteenth-century children's prayer is repeated nightly by millions of people throughout the world for their entire lives. The problem words are in the verse:

Now I lay me down to sleep,
I pray the Lord my soul to keep;
If I die before I wake,
I ask the Lord my soul to take.

His elderly nursing home residents were having difficulty sleeping. The words "if I should die before I wake" were causing the trouble. The elderly were unconsciously anxious they would die and have their souls taken away while they were asleep.

Wherever my hypnotherapist friend goes, he now teaches the elderly the following amended prayer:

Now I lay me down to sleep,
I pray the Lord my soul to keep.
Guide me through the coming night,
and wake me with the morning light.

The new prayer often removes their anxiety immediately and results in a better night's sleep.

Dictating Your First Dream

With all your organization completed, dictating your dreams will be easy. If you are like me, you will probably wake up from your first dream in the middle of the night. Check your alarm clock for the time, and go to your private place. You will be a little excited when you describe your first dream. Don't worry. Turn your voice recorder on, and narrate your dream from beginning to end in your normal voice and tempo. As you are going through the dream, more detail will pop into your head. Don't stop or go back. It is important you get the full dream from beginning to end in the right sequence. When you or your characters speak in the dream, be careful to use the exact words.

After the first narration, relax and take a moment to remember exactly what you missed the first time. Think about all the small details of the dream, the small objects you saw, the height of the rooms, and whether you turned left or right down that hallway. Think about the people and animals in your dream. How many were there? How old were they? What did they look like, and what were they wearing? How did they act during the dream? How many windows were there? What was that thing on the table? How did you feel when you woke up?

Say It Once, Think, Say It Again

The details of your dreams will help you later identify where your dream was happening and the present-day situation it was about. There is usually something out of place or something that does not belong in that dream setting. It could be something like a typewriter on a table at a cocktail party or someone wearing dress shoes while gardening. These will be important clues later on.

Once you are highly focused on all the minute details of the dream, narrate the dream again but much more slowly. It's OK this time to go back and forth in your dream sequence to make sure you get everything you remember. Rambling on and using run-on sentences is how I do my second run. Try to remain unemotional. Do not fill in any missing dream information. If there is a hole in the dream, just say so. Never improve the dream in any way.

Many dreams contain multiple breaks between them. If you have this type of dream, it is important you record the dream sequentially with the breaks noted. Wherever a dream breaks, it gives you a clue. Breaks usually happen at a high stress point. We have breaks in dreams when our unconscious wants to give us more detailed information than an average dream.

Some dreams are so fascinating and confusingly familiar we become fixated on them and cannot go back to sleep. We do not realize at the time we are incapable of understanding anything about the dream because we are still half asleep. I have done it myself many times. Do not get caught up in the dream's meaning after you have dictated it. Once you have all the facts recorded, turn off your recorder, and go back to bed. Trust your narration. Everything important has been saved. Think about something relaxing, and close your eyes. Your dream will become easily understood within a day or two.

Sometimes, when you wake up, you will only remember a small piece of a dream or even just a strong emotion. That's OK. Record the dream just as you would a normal dream. Sometimes a small memory or feeling will lead to much more valuable information later on.

Review the Dream, Fill Out the Form

Within a day or two of recording your dreams, you will need to combine both of your dream narratives into a single, complete version and answer a few important questions. I suggest you either attach or copy your final version to the top of a dream form, see page 80.

Be sure to always merge the second dream version into the first. Do not be tempted to do it the other way. By always retaining your original tape recording, you won't ever mix up the sequence of events. The final version does not have to be grammatically perfect or spell-checked. The most important things are accuracy, order and detail.

To summarize your dream for review, you will need to answer the following questions on your dream form.

1) Dream date and time

2) What do you want to name your dream?

The best way to create a memorable name is to start with a run-on sentence that describes the action. For example, I went to the fair with my dog and he found a body on the road and then bit my girlfriend. Now shorten the sentence to the most important action such as "Rover bit Mary at fair."

3) What is the real-life situation of the dream all about?

If you know for sure where the dream takes place and what it is about, answer this question. If not, don't guess. It's better to wait until later. Sooner or later the answer will pop into your mind. For example, "my presentation" or "dinner at Jim's."

4) Make a list of your dream characters by their emotional or action names, and record the level of

emotions they showed during the dream. List the characters with the most powerful emotions first, and then rate the intensity of their emotions from zero (for no emotion) to three (for very high emotion). Be sure to include yourself in the character list. If you had a large crowd of characters all acting the same way, write down how many there were, but treat them all as one person from an emotional standpoint.

a. Dream Character / Emotional Intensity

b. Dream Character / Emotional Intensity

c. Your Character / Emotional Intensity

5) How emotional were you after the dream? (0–3)

The intensity of your emotion after the dream is very important. Don't be shocked if you had no emotional reaction to a highly emotional dream or vice versa.

6) List any dream altering factors.

o Did you eat late the night before the dream?

o Did you drink too much alcohol or take mood-altering drugs?

o   Did you consume any greasy or unhealthy food before going to bed?

o   Did you sleep well that night?

o   Did anything emotional or unusual happen to you before you went to bed?

o   Was this a middle of the night dream?

Once you become used to summarizing your dreams, this activity should take you only twenty to thirty minutes a day. Your dreams may seem exclusively about something in the present, but they also carry important future meaning. This can be extremely useful value when you look back at them retroactively. That is another reason to save your dream forms as well as the taped recordings.

Think of your dream tonight as only a small part of a longer conversation between your unconscious core and your conscious mind. When you reread these conversations sequentially, your understanding and perspective of your unconscious will widen. Rereading your present dreams will also help harmonize your mind and resolve inner conflicts.

It is important to continue to record and summarize all your personal dreams into the dream form until the entire program is complete.

Chapter 5
Reviewing Dreams for Awareness, Suggestions, and Prophecies

From Reliable Dreams to Outright Lies

You have probably noticed the majority of your dreams are personal dreams. While we all dream about the same things, personal dreams take place only in our familiar environments and are concerned with everyday issues. That's why complex people produce more complex dreams, and world leaders have different dream landscapes than soldiers.

All personal dreams vary in value from totally reliable to outright, negative lies. The good news is most of your recorded personal dreams will contain some helpful information. You will also discover there is a lot more negative conflict going on inside your unconscious than you ever realized. Do not despair. This is expected. These dreams are always about a reality in your present-day life and can be positive or negative.

You didn't ask for these dreams. They arrived on their own to make you aware of something, encourage you to change your life goals, turn the direction of your actions, warn you of danger, show you a future filled with potential success, remind you of your ideals, help you make impossible decisions, or seek perfection. Feel free to get excited.

The Perfect You

One of the things that make us individuals is that we all get to choose our own values and ideals. We become more individual in our lives as we accumulate more qualities and ideals that are of additional value to us. What makes the dreams from our core useful is they are highly attuned to our values and ideals. Just as we instinctively learn to care for our body and seek excellent physical health, our core has its own drive to support the ideals and values we have consciously chosen in order to achieve perfection.

Your core always wants you to be your perfect ideal. It does that by creating dreams that make you aware of what you are doing and what will likely happen to you in the future. By reviewing your dreams, you will receive invaluable and otherwise unavailable information that supports your conscious values and ideals.

The Dreams of Sinners and Saints

You don't have to be a person with high values and ideals to benefit from your personal dreams. You don't even need to be a skilled interpreter of your personal symbols. You only have to be consistently honest. Everybody has the required skills. Everybody regularly receives these beneficial, personal dreams regardless of their ideals.

Some people think those with low ideals must have happier dreams than those with higher ideals. Theoretically, if you have lower ideals, your unconscious will have a lower standard of perfection, but I doubt your dreams will be any happier. Then there are those who live in constant fear of God's judgment. Are they so worried about their imperfections that they sleep less happily? I don't think so. I have also heard more than one highly religious person say that bad people are happier in their dreams because they are going to Hell anyway, and God wants them to enjoy themselves while on earth. I don't believe that either. I do know, however, that honest people have more reliable dreams, while liars and hypocrites have much more unreliable dreams.

Where Are You?

Personal dreams are very easy to review but only if you know the real-life situation being dreamed about. If you cannot place the dream situation, do not bother trying to review it. It will be entirely unreliable. You will find you cannot place some dreams, and other dreams contain no helpful information. Don't be disappointed. At best, you will get useful information from about half your personal dreams.

Example of an Awareness Dream
with a Suggestion

The following paragraph is an example of a simple, low-importance awareness dream with an indirect suggestion for a change in behavior. All sample dreams have been published with the express permission of the dreamer, de-identified, and edited for training purposes:

I was attending a fancy party in a very modern office building with high glass ceilings and a beautiful view of the city. I was feeling beautiful and wearing a very pretty blue dress with white pearls. There were more than fifty people there. I was standing next to my father, who was not paying attention to me.

Everyone was having a good time except me. No one was talking with me. In the corner was a young man playing the piano, and he kept smiling at me. I did not like him looking at me. Then the waiter came by and asked me if I wanted some champagne. I took the bottle from his tray and began to pour it all over my father's shoes. I was very frustrated and angry. No one, including my father, seemed to notice what I was doing.

Finding Awareness

This dream has an awareness message that the woman is behaving inappropriately without knowing it. "I took the bottle from his tray and began to pour it all over my father's shoes." She is not acting in accord with her own ideal of social behavior. Awareness dreams typically tell us we are too angry, aggressive, dependent, independent, or unhelpful. They may tell us we are not doing something often enough or aggressively enough. The value of all awareness dreams is our ability to make a quick adjustment based upon our new dream knowledge. If an awareness dream is positive, we get to build on that activity to make the future benefits even more positive and productive.

What Were the Emotions?

Like many less important, present-day dreams, this simple dream had no emotional impact on the dreamer afterward. She remembered, however, she was upset with her "father" character during the dream. While she clearly understood the real-life situation (a regional sales meeting), she was very surprised to learn she was "frustrated and angry." She was especially surprised by the indirect dream suggestion that she needed to be more open and social with her peers. "Everyone was having a good time except me. No one was talking with me." Her first reaction was to disagree with the message. Later she reconsidered and judged the message favorably.

Not Everything Is Important

While most personal dreams contain some valuable knowledge, not everything in the dream is useful. For example, the meaning of pouring champagne on the shoes, the unappreciated, smiling, young piano man, and the beautiful blue dress with pearls were not immediately understandable or beneficial. While a psychiatrist or psychologist may be able to help her uncover the meaning in these details, they are not necessary for her to gain beneficial information from the dream.

Imagine you went to see a foreign movie last week, but unfortunately it was neither dubbed nor subtitled. You did not understand the movie at all, and because it had no meaning, you forgot the movie immediately afterward. It did not affect you in any way. The same is true if you have an awareness dream you do not understand. Your life would proceed on its current course without change.

Prophecies and Warnings

While you frequently will find some element of prophecies in your awareness dreams, 100 percent pure prophecy dreams occur infrequently. I estimate it is only between 5 and 10 percent of the time. They are, however, an excellent source of future guidance and inspiration. Positive prophesies and negative prophesies, also called warning dreams, will lead you to a higher self-worth and a willingness to sacrifice something of lesser value to gain something superior.

Prophecy dreams are frequently more complicated than awareness dreams, and they require more focus to understand. Like all personal dreams, you must first understand the underlying real-life situation.

Once you are aware of that situation, then the prophecy becomes more obvious. Prophecy dreams are usually about a specific anticipation in your life, and if negative, they will always allow the time to improve what you are doing before that negative outcome occurs. Warning dreams do not punish us with hopeless negative judgments.

Example of a Prophecy Dream

The following dream is typical of a warning dream. Warning dreams may dare you to take some specific action, but they will not offer unrealistic or impractical advice. Our unconscious is always more aware than our conscious of how far we have come in our lives. As a result, many of our warning dreams have to do with our human tendency to overreach our capabilities.

I am driving into NYC, I think, in a newspaper delivery truck with large sliding front doors. I am sitting up high on a narrow seat without a belt. There is lots of traffic around me, and I'm in a big hurry. I'm going as fast as I can in the passing lane. There is a large red thermos bottle on the seat next to me. The engine is running loud. It sounds like it's going too fast. I want to pull over, but I cannot see out the back window, and there are no rearview mirrors. Then, from out of nowhere, a piece of metal flew into my left eye. I tried to rub it out, but my eye started tearing up, and I had a lot of trouble keeping my eyes on the road. The next thing I saw was a pile of gigantic rocks in front of me indicating the road was shut down. I tried to miss them, but I somewhat smashed up the front of the truck getting around them and just kept on going. Now I was the only one on the road. After a long turn to enter the tunnel, I got stuck in a traffic jam that wasn't moving. Then I realized I had a flat tire. When I woke up, I was worried.

The dreamer was very worried about this dream from the time he woke up at three a.m. The evening before this dream, he had gone out to dinner late, had a few drinks, and awakened several times during the night due to a gassy stomach. The dream seemed more emotional during the dream than afterward. I explained to him how his stomach problems made his dream less reliable.

The man with this dream figured out his real-life situation right away from the metal "chip" in his eye. He would soon be traveling to a large, metropolitan area to sell computer equipment. The prophecy dream certainly was negative. The core message was if he kept doing what he was doing, "going as fast as I can" something would fly into his eye and stop the sale. There was even more information. The dream suggested he was more focused on the "lots of traffic around" than in what was behind him. "I cannot see out the back window, and there are no rearview mirrors," By understanding his prophesy dream, he had the time to revise his proposed sales strategy for the meeting, and focus on the customers historical challenges and needs. Despite the negative prophesy, he got the sale.

Reliable Dreams

Personal dreams, just like our personal communication, are not always perfect. If we are sick with a fever, are overtired, eat too late at night, drink too much alcohol, take strong medication, or eat greasy, unhealthy food before going to bed, our dreams become significantly less reliable. Other signs of trouble include midnight dreams between fits of insomnia, high anxiety while still dreaming, and dreams that seem to wander from one subject to the next. These trouble signs indicate these dreams are not to be taken too seriously.

The most reliable and believable dreams from our core unconscious follow a familiar pattern. The dream usually occurs just after you fall asleep or just before you awaken. The dream is compact and lean, and it does not go off in unnecessary directions. While the dream actions and intensity are strong, clear, and vivid, you don't feel any emotions while you are dreaming. When you awaken, however, the post-dream emotion is strong. The closer your dream fits this profile, the more seriously it should be taken.

What do you do when you wake up feeling sad in the morning, but you cannot remember the dream? The first thing you should do is focus on your good behavior. It will also make you feel a lot better if you say a prayer, practice meditation, or do a few selfless acts of charity.

There is truth in the logic that the more important the dream, the more likely you are to remember it. Slightly less accurate is the inference that the more clear the dream, the sooner any predicted warning will take place. I can assure you that if you have a dream that is important enough, you will have a recurring dream soon after. Usually it will contain some character changes and maybe some more dream detail.

How Reliable Was Your First Dream?

If you are like me, you will find your earliest recorded dreams the most interesting. Let's open your first dream form and see what we can learn. The amount of emotion you felt after the dream is the prime indicator of the dream's importance. What was your answer to question number five?

According to classical Jewish dream interpretation, the reliability of the dream also has to do with the time of the dream and your environment before and during sleep. This is a subjective opinion. Only you can determine this based upon the circumstances.

As I mentioned before, dreams containing some element of prophecy occur frequently, while pure prophecy dreams happen less than 10 percent of the time. Whether the prophecy dream is good or bad, it is helpful to get some idea when this prophecy is going to happen. In prophesies the clearer and more vivid the dream, the sooner it will happen. An especially vivid prophecy may happen today, while a very faint dream may take more than a decade to happen.

When Will the Dream Prophecy Come True?

Whether the prophecy dream is negative or positive also affects when the prophecy will likely occur. Based on the theory that all present dreams will benefit the conscious mind, negative prophecies will always occur more quickly than positive dreams, especially if you are acting very badly at the time. The logic is sound. We either change our negative behavior or not. Knowledge of our need to become better in the future is not as useful as knowing we must become better right away. Giving us a lot of time to change our bad behavior can actually work against us. It allows us more time to fall back on old ways.

Positive dream prophecies work the opposite way. Your core is saying you can achieve this positive outcome in the future, but you need some time to work for it and earn the potentially good outcome.

In both cases, your beneficial unconscious is trying to help you the best way it can. By analyzing the type of dream and its clarity, you will need to estimate when you think this dream prophecy will come true. Use the zero to three scale, where zero indicates today, and three means some time in the distant future.

Because you have done all the hard work of organizing your dreams, searching for beneficial knowledge will be easy. Let's look at your first dream form again. Quickly read the dream and all details noted. As I mentioned before, the most challenging task in a dream review is figuring out what real-life situation is being acted out. Once you figure that out, the rest will be easy. Don't continue with this dream review until you identify the real-life situation.

I guarantee the dream subject will be important and contemporary, but uncovering the all-important dream location itself may require a little imagination. A good place to start is to write down the most important things going on in your life. Could any of these situations take place in this dream location?

You can usually separate your business locations from the personal ones. The next clue is usually the number of characters or large objects in the dream. If there are three characters or two buildings, what real-life place has three people or two buildings? The answer is soon going to pop out at you, and you will laugh at how obvious it is. Everything that was nonsensical in the dream will become clear.

If you still are not there yet, look for the unusual object in your dream. This will be something that does not belong in that dream setting. Where does this type of object belong? If there is physical action in the dream, mimic the action, and think about where you move like that. Where do you walk into a large room, go to the back, and take a left turn to an office? Pay attention to the exact words of your characters. Do any of those words have more than one meaning? Does a strange dream name such as "St. Mark," when combined with another letter or two, spell out a real name such as Mary Kennedy, your highly religious friend?

You know this dream place. It is a real place, and you have been there before. It is altered and exaggerated in your unconscious, but you know exactly where it is. If you cannot figure it out, read the dream every night before you go to bed. Within a day or two, you will figure it out 95 percent of the time. In rare cases, it may take several months to solve. This is fun, creative work. Until you are sure of the dream location and situation, I want you to move on to your next dream. You cannot mine a dream accurately without knowing the location and situation.

How to Measure Dream Importance

On your dream form, you need to summarize each character's emotion, including your own, during the dream. For example, I was feeling 1 angry and 2 jealous during the dream. The advantage of rating each character is to understand the relative importance of each emotion. Remember, the purpose of the dream is to help you improve your life. Having multiple emotions during the dream suggests you may need to find ways to deal with those feelings.

The emotion after the dream, however, is what is most important. It tells you how important the dream is. A dream where you felt 1 angry afterward is less important than a dream where you felt 3 angry.

Finding the Suggestion

Now look for the suggestion. Many awareness dreams contain a hidden suggestion to make your life better. After you uncover the awareness problem, the suggestion is much easier to find. It is usually something someone says during the dream, some activity people are doing, or an unusual choice of words describing what they did. For example, someone says, "So I left," "everyone was exercising," or "John was wearing a new suit." Your core may be suggesting you leave, exercise or buy a new suit.

When you combine the awareness with the suggestion, you will have received most of the beneficial meaning of your awareness dream. In many of these dreams, there is also a hint of prophecy. By itself it will not be evident, but as you continue to read the dream, the prophesy will pop out at you. This is where dream experience helps.

I strongly suggest you do not automatically accept any dream suggestion. You have to look at the dream situation and the reliability of the dream. Then you can make your own evaluation of how correct the advice is. Assuming a dream is reliable however, you'll probably find these suggestions to be excellent. Even so, you cannot allow your unconscious to make decisions for you. You must consciously decide whether you agree with the dream suggestion, and then do what you think is best.

You may have discovered that your first dream is not an awareness dream. If that is the case, it could be a prophecy dream. A prophecy dream is usually an action dream that takes place in the future. The dream is showing you what will happen if things continue the way they are. This can be either a positive or a negative prophecy. The dream never says your future is fixed. The fact you are having the dream indicates the prediction is not fixed in stone.

Just as in an awareness dream, there is usually a suggestion with a prophecy. With your knowledge of the place and situation, the negative or positive prophecy suggestion should be easy to find. You must exercise special care with these types of dreams. Your unconscious produces fantasy dreams that look like prophecy dreams. Never change your life based solely upon a dream!

Now that you understand dream awareness, prophesy and suggestions, you should be able to review each of your dreams using the following dream form.

Narrative:

1) Date and time

2) Dream name

3) Real-life situation

4) Characters and emotions in dream

    o Character / Emotional Intensity
    o Character / Emotional Intensity
    o Character / Emotional Intensity

5) Dream importance

6) Reliability

    o Eat late
    o Alcohol or drugs

- ○ Greasy or unhealthy food
- ○ Sleep well
- ○ Emotional or unusual before bed
- ○ Middle of the night dream

7) Awareness

8) Prophesy

9) When

10) Suggestion

What to Do About a Negative Prophecy

So let's say you have a negative prophecy dream about a meeting you will have next week. During the dream, you get shot with a pistol by one of the dream characters. Let's also assume it was a reliable dream. You woke up after the dream, and you were very upset and depressed. What should you do?

The dream is suggesting there is more going on than you are aware. You need to rethink the meeting and become better prepared for any eventuality. You should also look inside the dream for suggestions and clues, as you do in awareness dreams. You may find an outside character that is not you in your dream.

His or her behavior may provide a clue. The dream action itself, being shot, may also be a clue.

Sometimes what appears impossible to change in a future situation is just a matter of perspective and putting yourself in someone else's shoes. Other times you need to surround the problem continuously with your thoughts to come up with a creative solution. A negative prophecy dream is a tremendous gift. It should not provoke you to take an immediate action. It should provoke reconsideration of what you are doing and why. It may well lead to a change of your intentions and strategy.

Be Careful with Your Prophecy Dreams

You always need to ask yourself many questions when dealing with a prophecy. Is the suggestion ethical? What will happen to everyone else if I change what I'm doing? Can anyone be hurt? Your dreams should never suggest you do anything that could hurt you or anyone else. Whenever you deal with your unconscious, you must always be careful to make your own detailed rational analysis of the situation, as you will be responsible for your own decisions.

Positive Prophecies Always Need Your Help

Positive prophecy dreams require the same amount of scrutiny as negative ones. For example, you suddenly start to dream romantically about someone with whom you work. In your dreams, you are madly in love with this person and in an ideal relationship. There's just one problem. You are married.

Your collective unconscious can create very strong fantasy images that can dominate your dreams. These dreams may look like positive prophecy dreams, but they are actually dangerous collective dreams. You know this because you realize the urge is in direct conflict with your ideals. Your moral conscience would never suggest this future because that is not who you are. Your primitive collective unconscious, however, is frequently in conflict with your ideals and values.

Both positive and negative prophecy dreams require us to reconsider what we're doing. In the case of positive prophecies, we need to strongly consider those future actions that can actively support the positive prophecy. The positive prophecy dream also suggests that, if we do not support the positive future outcome, it may not ever happen.

If you do nothing with your awareness and prophecy dreams other than reread them, you will still receive the substantial benefit of improved communication with your unconscious. Rereading is a short, simple, honest, practical, symbolic, and supportive act. By associating with the dream, you support your conscious to unconscious harmony and gain insight into your behavior.

Always consciously acknowledge before reading your dreams that you will never give up your values and beliefs. The goal of dream reviews and rereading is to affirm, accept, recognize, and reinforce your ideals. Over time, your dream recollections will connect more clearly with your conscious mind. The more frequently you read your dreams, the more you will understand them. Keep in mind that, many times, the dream is doing what you should be doing in order to be more independent.

Chapter 6
Tough Decisions

What You Value

One of the best ways to understand who you are is to understand what you value. This chapter requires you to identify and review the most difficult events and decisions you have experienced in your life. In order to reexamine past events, you will need the active support of your core unconscious, which you are learning more and more about in this program.

No Rejudging

You are not going to be rejudging the choices you have made in the past. Your past no longer exists. It happened. That is true and factual, but it is no longer objective. Whenever you look into the past, you are unavoidably viewing it subjectively.

True Motivations

What you are looking for are the true motivations for what you did and how these decisions affected your life. Your motivations will reveal the background story of who you are. By looking into your past, there is also a secondary benefit of increasing your dream production.

An Unexamined Life

Socrates is credited with the statement, "The unexamined life is not worth living." He believed that, without understanding who we are, we could not begin to fulfill the meaning of our lives. Another philosopher, Santayana, expanded the idea with his famous quotation, "He who does not remember the past is condemned to repeat it." This is the perfect time to do this important work. Because you are working entirely on your own, there is no need to hide any aspect of your life. I personally found my examination of past decisions to be the most valuable in opening up.

The Emotional Events Are Tough

In this exercise, you are going to identify the most difficult events and decisions of your life. Then you will analyze what you did and, most importantly, why you did it. These highly emotional events are the building blocks that make you who you are, and they are essential to your human experience. To better understand yourself as a whole person, this exercise will also help you tie together all the previously considered unrelated events of your life.

Please be as objective as possible. Facing a sometimes-uncomfortable truth requires enormous care, patience, and most of all, courage. This exercise is not simple or easy. It will probably be the most time-consuming but most rewarding of the exercises you will perform. When you have completed the exercise, you will treasure the final product and save it. I know you will return to it frequently for years to come, especially in times of personal conflict.

Stuck in the Middle Period

Think of your total self-development as analogous to building a home. The first parts of construction are digging the basement and pouring the foundation, and they are critically important. They progress quickly, however, as does childhood. It is in the middle of home construction and in the middle of our lives that the skilled work is accomplished. It usually only advances though, in fits and starts.

The middle period is the value-added part of home construction and of human development as well. In both construction and life we experience great frustration when we cannot go ahead with one important project until the preceding one is completed. These can be the most unpredictable time of our lives. People and events challenge us and continue to besiege us. As a result we feel more off-balance and unsettled.

For some of us, it feels as if we are always behind where we should be. Everything takes more time than expected. Nothing makes us feel more miserable than looking back and feeling we squandered an opportunity to do a better job at a given time.

Your Intentions Don't Matter

It has been said that the road to Hell is paved with good intentions. I would argue the road to Hell is downhill if you make your decisions with inferior motivations. All our best decisions are based upon our best values and ideals. Motivations are at the core of this exercise. If we are not even aware of our motivations when we make a decision, who is responsible for the decision? We have no hope of being responsible for our actions unless we consciously understand our motivations first. Unfortunately most of us have never bothered to reconsider our motivations once a decision is made.

Have you ever tried to punish someone by doing something deliberately to him or her, but the end result was you ended up helping that person? Have you ever acted in your own selfish interest only to accidentally help another person get what you wanted? How about the time you tried to help another person by doing something good, but your actions backfired, and you actually hurt the person. There are so many situations where we have little or no control that it seems as if we have no responsibility for our actions. But in highly emotional, critical situations, that is not usually true. In these cases, we are right in the middle of the action and significantly responsible for the outcome. These are the situations where motivations matter.

Make a List of Tough Decisions

Start by making a list of the most difficult events and decisions of your life. Just list them as you remember them in no particular order. Don't combine your tough decisions. A divorce, for example, is usually two or three tough decisions rather than just one. Ideally you will have more than twenty-five events. You need a minimum of twenty. The more events you have, the more the exercise will help you.

Most difficult decisions generally concern changes in key relationships, health problems, our children, work, finances, and legal matters. Starting with this year, slowly work your way backward to make sure you included everything. If you are like me, expect to be adding events to your list for several weeks to come. The events you add later on are usually the most important ones.

When Is Important

The next step is to write down the year of each decision. If you have a gap in your list with no decisions for several years, you may be repressing some of your past memories. Pay especially close attention to where you were and what you were doing during any gaps in time.

The timeline is mandatory. Associating an event with other events, favorite songs, or movies can usually help you remember when an event took place. Do not go to anyone you know for help in recollecting missing information. Opening up is strictly a private endeavor. You need to do all the memory work. If you want, you can enter more information than the worksheet project requires, but please hold off for now. It is important that whatever you list is as accurate and objective as possible.

What Really Happened?

Go get your digital recorder or pad of paper, and find your comfortable workplace. Think about your most recent difficult event from a factual point of view. Do not consider it from an emotional standpoint. You will need to challenge your memories of the event in order to become an honest reporter. Remind yourself you are good person, and promise yourself you will only narrate the truth. If you do lie, or even stretch the truth a little, your inner conscience will know and judge you poorly. Do the best you can, and realize your recall is affected by the passage of time. Trauma, health issues, and emotional events can also change your memories.

Narrate or write down the difficult situation the same way you narrated your dreams. First tell the story from beginning to end. Then repeat the story, if necessary, a second time with all the important details you may have left out. Be sure to include the event's outcome and whether you feel, in retrospect, your decision was successful.

Find the Central Conflict

When you are through dictating your first tough event, look for the central conflict. All difficult events contain critical conflicts. If you have multiple, unrelated conflicts, you may have to make the situation two decisions instead of one. Make sure your narrative contains a clear description of the central conflict along with your resolution options at that time. Tough decisions usually contain ethical conflicts.

When we attempt to make a decision that is contrary to our values, we feel conflicted. It does not matter where the conflict comes from. Whether it stems from another ideal or from an unconscious emotion, we feel as if we are mentally wrestling with ourselves. Our toughest decisions usually involve superior conflicts. They involve the conflict of our highest ideals.

We all understand what we value, but most of us do not take the time to confirm the right names for those ideals. If you feel strongly about something, look up the word you think describes it in the dictionary. Make sure you are using the right ideal or value to describe your conflicts. You may also find out many of your conflicts did not come from conflicting ideals. Many conflicts will come from the urges and desires of your collective unconscious.

Boiling down a difficult situation into conflicting ideals and motivations is hard. It would be a lot easier if you were not emotionally involved in the situation. In many of these situations, you simply did not know the best answer or how to find out what that best answer was. When you add the strong, unrelenting passions of your personal unconscious, you understand why you were facing such a tough decision.

You may start describing the conflict as, "who is more important: my children or my husband?" Later you may realize the real conflict is much deeper. The motivation for your final decision is usually your best clue to the real conflict. When you are finished, read the following rules of objectivity regarding tough decisions, and make whatever changes are required in your event dictations.

Did You Break the Rules of Objectivity?

Before you go any further, review the following rules of objectivity to make sure you are being as honest and open as possible.

Rules of Objectivity

1. Delete everything in your event narrative based upon third-party information. Hearsay is information you received from someone who was not a direct source of knowledge (e.g., they did not witness the event).

2. Delete all your subjective opinions and judgments.

3. No irrelevant details are allowed. For example, someone's ethnicity is almost always irrelevant.

4. Make no reference to making mistakes or doing things accidentally. No excuses are allowed.

5. Ask yourself directly, "Am I responsible for the event and what happened?" It's vitally important that you answer honestly. If you accept full responsibility, skip steps six through ten, and complete your answers to the ten important questions that follow.

6. If you deny responsibility, identify who you think was responsible. Give his/her name and why you think he/she was responsible.

7. Ask yourself, "Do you share any responsibility with anyone?"

8. If you accept any responsibility, narrate exactly what you were responsible for. Then narrate what would have happened if you had changed your behavior.

9. If you think you had no responsibility, justify why not. You need to identify that specific reason. For example, I was not there.

10. If you have raised a justification, reframe it from the opposite perspective. For example, am I responsible because I was not there?

The Important Questions
About Your Decision

When you are done, answer the following ten questions for each tough decision.

1. Give your decision a name.

2. When did it happen?

3. What was the central conflict?

4. Who was responsible for the conflict?

5. What was my decisive action? What did I do?

6. What was my true motivation for the decision?

7. Was my true motivation rational, emotional, or balanced?

8. Was the final outcome of my decision positive or negative?

9. If I showed positive, ideal behavior what was it?

10. If I showed negative behavior what was it?

You May Feel Disappointed

After completing an event narration, you may temporarily feel a little disappointed with yourself. Within a few days, however, you will feel rejuvenated again. I promise. Reliving old emotions can be exhausting. Many times we discover we never took appropriate responsibility for our past decisions and actions. We inappropriately gave someone else the authority and power to make decisions for us. This happens frequently in marriages when one person makes all key decisions. Many of us give too much authority to our doctors. Some people give up moral responsibility to gurus, teachers, and religious leaders.

Some of your events will demonstrate your best qualities, while others will not. If you find yourself getting upset, take a break and rest for a few moments before starting again. Remember, you love yourself. You're doing this for yourself. You only want to understand the truth. You're working on your own. No one is going to know the truth. We all make mistakes. We all do good things occasionally for the wrong reasons. Maybe you felt you had no choice. No one will judge you or think less of you in this program. It is just you who needs to know what you were responsible for.

If we function without full responsibility for what we do, then we cannot grow, learn, evolve, or avoid the same trouble in the future. By following the rules of objectivity, you have already demonstrated how fair-minded you are in your recollections of the past. We cannot deny our responsibilities while working with our conscience.

Our conscience is with us all the time, and it sees everything we do and say. Our conscience knows the objective truth. You will begin to understand over time whether your core respects you or not. If you consciously lie to yourself or frequently act hypocritically, you will find an undertone of sarcasm in your dreams. If your conscience does not respect you at all, it will ignore you and consider you a lost person.

Evidence of Ideals and Emotions

Besides what you did, how you implemented your decisions may reveal signs of positive or negative personal characteristics. You may find evidence of courage, compassion, unselfishness, and initiative in your actions, or you may find negative characteristics such as passivity, inferiority, and hostility. Whatever you find is a part of who you are. These are your strengths and weaknesses. We cannot unwind who we are.

Your Issues Are Revealed

As you process more tough decisions, you will find your life issues recurring frequently. You may be familiar with your issues but not realize how frequently you face them. You will also uncover small issues that only pop up in specific situations. You know where these sensitivities come from, and you have probably tried to resolve them over the years. You may have been able to compensate for these issues and achieved remarkable things in your life, but you cannot deny your issues exist. Unfortunately, because your conscience is fascinated with your values, ideals, responsibility, and personal honesty, you will continue to run into these issues in the future. Count on it.

There is an indirect benefit from examining the past. Because our memory is affected by the present, we always catch a glimmer of who we were then versus who we are now. If you could put your work in a time capsule for ten years and then reread it, you would see even more than you do today. Besides connecting the unrelated dots of your life, you are looking for the trajectory of good and bad. If you examine your decisions sequentially, you will begin to see where you have been heading.

Classify Your Decision

One of the most stunning results of this exercise is that we realize how influential our emotional unconscious has been in our decision-making processes. How many of your tough decisions were made for purely emotional reasons? If one of your true motivations was emotional, it came from your unconscious. If you had no emotional consideration, your motive came from the conscious. If you truly listened to both sides equally and made your decision based upon what was best for both, you made a balanced decision.

You should, therefore, have three types of motivations listed on your summary decisions page: rational only, emotional only, and balanced. You probably never thought about it before, but laziness is one of the most powerful negative motivations from your collective unconscious. You may be like me. My personal tough decision summary showed some disappointing evidence of laziness.

While the unconscious is very important in all decision-making, unconscious motivations are notoriously troublesome by themselves. Your conscious motivations are important, but also very unreliable without help from the unconscious. I suggest you do a quick tally of all the outcomes of your decisions based upon your motivations. Your best decisions are usually those where you used both your conscious and your unconscious core knowledge to resolve the problem. One of the goals of this book is showing you the benefits of using both your conscious and inner core cooperatively in all decision-making.

When you are in a tough situation requiring a difficult decision, you are usually suffering emotionally. Awareness of where your emotions are coming from will help. While you cannot control what you feel, accepting the emotion as a collective human condition will make you stronger. While your first instinct may be to either surrender to the urge or totally ignore it, I suggest learning to tolerate it while acknowledging you are in the grip of an unconscious event. You need to understand the emotion and why you are feeling it at this time. Look for the hidden knowledge. The collective urge may be extreme or grossly exaggerated just to get your attention.

Importance of Understanding

Understanding is the most effective tool for opening up. It gives us the necessary control over our emotions, which then allows us to consistently work as partners with our moral unconscious to achieve our life goals. It is the hard-won ability to love and accept your true self. Working hard at understanding is the only way your conscious mind can consistently resist the pull of the emotional unconscious.

Dealing with the Unconscious

This exercise has required you seeing yourself as separate from your unconscious. You must first be in control to accomplish difficult things. Knowing you can control and reject your collective unconscious makes you stronger. The stronger you become, the better you can analyze and understand what is happening within your unconscious. You can then begin to benefit from your unconscious. First you must experience separation. Then, with understanding, there can be reconciliation with your unconscious.

The more familiar you become with your conscience, the more aware you will be of its underlying critical nature. Our unconscious is fascinated with our values, ideals, responsibility, and personal honesty. The more we value something, the more likely we will be challenged by our conscience to prove it. If we cherish being a parent more than anything, we can be sure our children will dominate our life struggles.

What You Can't Do

Conflicts with your collective unconscious can be downright frightening. While there are a few things we can do to improve conflicts with our personal unconscious, there's nothing you can do to change your powerful collective unconscious. Slowly changing your attitude toward your unconscious based upon experience and trust is the most effective approach to gaining harmony. Despite our occasional suffering, we need the positive wisdom and insights of our unconscious, especially dealing with our chaotic and novel lives. The only requirement for allowing your conscious and unconscious to work together is that you must always be honest and responsible for your actions.

The More You Give the More You Get

Looking over the results of your tough decisions, you'll find that the more effort put into that exercise, the more benefits you'll receive by reexamining it. While this exercise was, in large part, about the process of reconstructing important moments in your life, it required you to work consistently with your conscience in an honest and open way. If you keep these narratives and reexamine them in the future, you will find your understanding of the past will change as you change.

Reward Yourself Alone

When you are sure every difficult event in your life has been recorded and processed, do something special for yourself. You deserve a reward. Preferably it will be a pleasurable physical reward for your hard mental work. I am truly proud of you. If you decide to celebrate by going out to dinner, however, be sure to celebrate alone. Opening up is a personal experience not a social experience. No sharing or discussion of your achievement is allowed.

By now your dreams should be getting much more interesting and possibly even more vivid. Once again, resist the urge to interpret your dreams and continue your dream logging and dream reviews.

Finally, this is a good time to review your goals and think about what questions you have for your core. Again, congratulations!

Chapter 7
Heroes and Role Models

Our Ideals and Values

We are all unique because we have different ideals. These ideals are sets of internal rules for correct behavior, which we try to follow under all circumstances. Ideals always create principles that limit our choices in life. We don't follow our individual ideals because we believe the ideal itself is so valuable. It is because we want the benefits of living according to the ideal. Without a benefit, however, the ideal loses its importance over time.

To complicate matters, we all have different ideals and rules. It is very human to see another person's principles and rules as inferior to our own, without any thought of their viewpoint. To accurately compare our values and ideals to another person's, we would both have to agree on how we define our ideals. Just as we all have different dream languages, we have different interpretations of our ideals and complementary moral language. Just because we agree on many things, doesn't mean we are truly alike. We all are uncommon, unique individuals.

We receive many of our ideals and values from the people we most honor and respect in our lives. Our values are always accepted after first experiencing the need for a specific, positive benefit. We then observe someone demonstrating the ideal in action, which then clearly produces the desired reward. Unless we later discover a superior role model, that person remains the best example of our ideal. This person becomes our hero or role model.

Heroes and Role Models

Our heroes and role models always exemplify an ideal behavior or value. The closer someone in your life comes to your total ideals, the more you value them. As we mirror our individual role models, we notice others mirroring us. They usually become our close friends.

Our Life Mission

Our highest ideals also create an unconscious, ideal direction for our lives. They lead us into action. You can see this at work in your everyday life. If you ever set a goal that is attached to a high, emotional ideal, and you work to attain the goal, your goal will take hold of you. You will become in some ways possessed by it. Your ideals will compel you to succeed. The value in examining your ideals lies in understanding your individual, unconscious myth.

Everyone has a life story. This is a journey we undertake unconsciously to fulfill our true nature. One of the best ways to uncover your nature is to understand your ideals. By connecting your ideals to your best intentions, you can uncover the true goal of your life. Rarely do any of us achieve all the goals of our life, but our ideals can illuminate the way. Ideals tell us about our potential. They provide us with a look forward, just as dreams help us remain true to our purpose.

No One Is Perfect

The people we idealize are not perfect. They usually have only one or two ideals we admire. If we look deeper into their characters, we find they have many imperfections, despite the exceptional quality of the admired ideals. As a result we cherry-pick only the ideal quality we want, and then we work hard to absorb it into the other ideals we acquired from others. We create for ourselves a mythical picture of our human perfection. While this creates conflicts between our conscious ideal and who really we are, it also gives us a clue to our purpose in life.

Ideals and Heroes Come from a Need in Time

Because our heroes and role models come to us when we are looking for a specific benefit, you may find these people by your side in your history of tough decisions. When you think about the most important people in your life, you likely will discover they were there in times of need or when an ideal action was required.

In this workshop, I want you to identify all the heroes and role models in your life. The only rule is they need be real people you know or once knew. Do not include historical or literary figures such as Jesus Christ or Robin Hood. Our true heroes and idols are like us: perfect in some ways but mostly imperfect human beings.

At some point, these special people were there for us in an important way. It is not important to this exercise if your hero later disappointed you in some way or even if you no longer like him or her. What is important is that all of these people entered your life and demonstrated an ideal or value you have incorporated into who you are or who you want to be.

Make a list of the people you have most admired in your life and why. Just as with your personal history, start in the present, and go back one year at a time. On your notes, be sure to write down why you admire that person so much. Don't be concerned if you know these people very well or if you have a long or a short list. After you have completed your list, review your tough decision narratives. Think about anyone you may have missed. Sometimes we don't even notice where our ideals come from.

I have a friend who is very outgoing and charming to everyone he meets. He tries to emotionally connect with everyone he comes in contact with and does a great deal of charitable work. When I am with him, I marvel at how much happiness and inspiration he brings to so many people. However, for all his good points, he is also at times a judgmental, and distrustful person. Regardless of his faults, he will always be my idol and hero for sociability.

The next step is to transform why that person is your hero into an ideal or value he/she represents. If you are unsure of the exact definition of the ideal, look it up on the Internet. If there is more than one ideal, write them both down.

The final step in this exercise is to reread your tough decision narratives one more time to identify evidence of times when you were a hero in your own life. These are situations when you acted upon your highest ideals and remained true to your positive nature. You need to add yourself to the hero list. Be sure to add why this is so and your clearly defined ideals

Once you have completed this section, summarize all your ideals into a short, declarative narrative. In your own words, describe someone with all the ideals of your heroes and role models including all your own well demonstrated ideals. The narrative will capture the truth of who you are and who you were born to become. It is the positive projection of yourself.

Make sure you keep up your dream work throughout the entire program, and be sure to continue saying your bedtime memory suggestion.

Chapter 8
People I Avoid

An Instinctive Dislike

Just as we have people we honor or respect in our lives, there are others we strongly, almost instinctively, dislike. These are the people who don't like us and seem to enjoy every opportunity to cause us trouble and hold us back. They frequently have questionable ethics, insult us in public, and tell lies about us when we are not around. They are usually unscrupulous and tricky. They make us feel frustrated and, on some occasions, quite angry.

The goal of this exercise is to identify all the people who have been significant adversaries in your life or who drain you emotionally whenever you are with them. I call them the "people I avoid."

Most of the difficult people we know are forced upon us without our consent. They are coworkers, spouses of good friends, next-door neighbors, and family members. We don't like them any more than they like us. We feel frustrated when we are with them, and there is always an undercurrent of difficult emotions. These people steal our energy and hijack our environment. They may have been bothering us for a while now.

I am not talking about individuals we prefer not to spend time with and never think about. Our enemies are like an open wound. They are never far away and always provide some discomfort to us. They can be very clever in hiding who they are in order to be popular. They may seem very nice when you first meet them, but later on you discover they are anything but.

If someone drains you emotionally, you really dislike him/her, or you see him/her as a bad example of something important, put that person on your "persons I avoid" list. Like your idols and heroes list, only real people you know or once knew belong on this particular list.

In your notes, add why you dislike these people so much. Don't be concerned if you do not know them very well or if you have a long or short list. It does not matter if they have other redeeming qualities, or if you love them on some level. If they meet the qualification for a "person you avoid," put them on the list. After you have completed your list, try to boil down the reason you don't like each person to a specific fault or missing moral standard. If there are multiple reasons, list them all.

Defense Mechanisms

It may surprise you to learn that most, if not all, of the people you listed are there because of your unconscious. Projection is a common psychological defense mechanism used by our unconscious to compensate for negative feelings and emotions. These negative feelings and emotions are hiding in our unconscious. Projection happens when we unconsciously project negative emotions onto another person rather than admitting we also have these emotions. It makes us feel better to reject the feelings we secretly feel. There is no conscious decision to reject the unwanted emotion and project it, and it never occurs to us we are being unconsciously hypocritical. Because we are unaware of what we are doing, we have no defense against ourselves.

Projection

The theory of psychological projection was developed by Sigmund Freud and is sometimes called "Freudian projection." Freud noticed during therapy that his patients would accuse others of the feelings they had themselves. The patient was better able to deal with their emotions by projecting them. A classic case of projection is that of a man who has been unfaithful to his wife but continually accuses his wife of cheating on him. By consciously believing only others are bad, we convince ourselves we are good people.

Not everyone on your list will be a case of projection. There are truly evil people in the world. These are dangerous and harmful personalities we need to avoid and protect ourselves from. We can also be recipients of projection with or without participating in it. The work required in this exercise is to examine the people you avoid for any evidence of projection.

Clues You Are Projecting

One clue you may be projecting is when no one else sees the other person's behavior the same way you do. Looking for areas where we are similar to those people we don't like may be hard, but it can be extremely rewarding. Your projection makes you feel vaguely unhappy in this person's company, and it drains you of valuable mental energy. This is where it helps to work on your own. You don't have to share anything you discover in this exercise with anyone.

Another place to find evidence of projection is within your difficult decisions file. Just as our ideals come to us within a specific situation and time, our dark, unconscious side is also created within specific situations and time. If you could recall when you first had negative feelings for a person, the root cause of your projection would be much easier to understand. Jung called our unconscious weaknesses and shortcomings our "shadow." We all have trouble accepting our shadow, and when we do, it is an unpleasant and drawn-out experience.

Like a good detective, take another look at your difficult decisions. If you find evidence of something unpleasant about yourself, spend time looking for more corroborating proof. Where you find shadow behavior, it will likely be repeated in many negative experiences. It will provide a behavioral thread linking what you previously thought were unrelated events. Can you find your shadow in any of the people you avoid? For most of us, our shadow contains, at the minimum, the most common human frailties. We all can be lazy, selfish, controlling, and childish on occasion.

If you focus on the essence of why you dislike a particular person, you will always find a part of yourself. Ask yourself the question, "Have I ever been ------?" It may not be immediately obvious, but after scouring your long-term memory, you will experience an aha moment. The moment you discover you have projected your shadow behavior onto another person whom you avoid will not be a happy one.

"Repression" is the psychological term for shutting unwanted thoughts out of our consciousness. Our repressed thoughts don't go away. They stay with us in our unconscious. Jung suggested unconscious repression takes substantial energy. By releasing repressed material, we can release energy that will then become available for other mental activities. We are always astonished to find what we hide from ourselves. Initially you may feel emotionally deflated and somewhat humble, but after only a few days, you probably will feel very relieved and much happier.

Overcoming Projection

Once you accept you have been projecting, the habit does not just disappear. You will have to be aware of this tendency in your future relationships. There are three aspects to repairing your tendency toward projection: acknowledgement, dealing with what was formerly your shadow behavior, and a plan to better deal with others in the future. Only when you accept and acknowledge your negative issues can you begin to change and heal.

Go easy on yourself. You did not know what you were doing. You are not a hypocrite. Your shadow feelings are universal human faults. They are not evil thinking. You are not alone in your imperfections. By accepting your shadow and living with it, you will be a more loving and loveable human being going forward. Welcome to the human race.

The key to controlling your past projection is understanding what situations triggered your need to defend yourself. If you prepare yourself in advance for these situations, you can better handle them in a positive way. Your old projections get in the way of your sociability, and they limit your relationships to people who also project. We frequently alienate ourselves from the people we most need to understand and accept.

You don't fully know it yet, but your newfound knowledge is going to make you a better, stronger, and happier person. Keep in mind that opening up is a process, and there is much more to see and understand.

By uncovering our unconscious ideals and shadow, we begin to understand our hidden nature. By making this material conscious, we release energy and can learn to consciously deal with the undesirable behavior. As long as our projections remain hidden, we will have inexplicable and uncontrollable conflicts with our goals and ideals. To complicate matters, your unconscious cannot be easily changed.

After you gain awareness of your hidden shadow, you need to accept it. Then you must develop a strategy to allow your negative emotions to peacefully exist with your ideals in order to reduce conflicts. Conscious recognition of our impulses makes us aware of our imperfections and more tolerant. When we learn not to put others in a negative situation, we are more likely to receive help from them when we are in need of support. As you become more open, you will automatically look for and dismantle any newly discovered projections.

The final step to healing projection is acknowledging the negative behavior by deliberately doing something physical. For example, after careful detective work, you realize you have been punishing someone or even multiple people over many years in certain similar situations. When you were younger, you were unfairly punished. You wanted to punish your punisher but were unsuccessful. The projection started later in life when you reacted to someone that reminded you of your past punisher.

Acknowledgement of shadow behavior requires action. You could release a large part of your now-conscious negative feelings by performing a simple act of kindness for the person you victimized. You could also do this kindness for a stranger who was victimized by someone else. Do not, however, turn your physical acknowledgement into a big apology. As our parents taught us, actions speak louder than words. You do not owe anyone a public confession.

Your action here should be short and to the point. We all have faults. It is a good thing to go forward with your life and look out for these negative feelings in the future, but be careful. Projection will come back if you don't pay attention.

Now return to your tough events summary, and review those negative personal characteristics you listed in the questionnaire. These are negative qualities you uncovered in difficult situations. They may have negatively influenced a decision in your life. You need to add these inferior qualities to your avoid list under your own name.

Once you have completed this section, summarize all your shadow instincts in a short, declarative narrative. Make sure you have included all of them.

The narrative will show you which negative aspects of your collective unconscious you are most vulnerable to. These emotions are the ones with the greatest potential to keep you from achieving what you want in life.

Chapter 9
Reinforcing and Bridging to Resolve Conflicts

The Unconscious Is Intractable

By opening up, you are becoming more aware of the important conflicts between your conscious, ideal mind and your emotional unconscious. These conflicts are often serious and an ever-present obstacle to achieving your life goals. The reason these problems are so intractable is that your unconscious is very difficult to change.

The goal of this chapter is to offer several proven strategies to help you better resolve these conflicts. While they will help you deal with most everyday conflicts, they are not always effective, especially if you are experiencing highly emotional conflicts. If these techniques do not work the first time, repeat them but using a different approach.

The Goal of Releasing Energy

Imagine the tension created between your ideals and conflicting emotions as a short spring attached to two screws on a wall. The greater the distance between ideals and conflicting emotions, the more the spring will stretch. As a result, more tension will be created. You need to ease your internal conflicts without changing your ethics. Opening up is like a spring that allows you to release the tension of unconscious energy, remain focused, adapt, and solve complicated problems. Go slowly to achieve the very best results.

Conflicts affect your actions, relationships, decisions, feelings, and even your loyalties. We all have these conflicts, so do not be surprised if you have more than one. Your unwanted and persistent conflicts can be very unlike who you are in any material and essential way. These conflicts complicate your life and create unnecessary stress. Without conflict, our dreams become gentler and our decisions more wise. Our unconscious goes on vacation.

The Source of Your Conflicts

This is a good time to acknowledge the source of your conflicts. I bet that most, if not all, of your conflicts come from your collective, primitive impulses and emotions. These are the very same dream impulses and emotions we rejected and refused to deal with throughout the dream review process. These conflicts are not about you. They come from all of mankind throughout all time. These urges cannot be eliminated or rationalized away. Here we see the true source of our fears, anxiety, and also compassion. There is no reason to get upset about these impulses. They are part of our humanity. Our best coping strategy is to accept each impulse without acting on it, despite the negative tension it creates within us.

Classify Your Conflicts

Think of your conflicts in terms of their frequency and importance. Recurring conflicts are the most serious. They are your "issues." Next in severity are conflicts that have recurred but only in unique situations such as business matters or playing a sport. One-time conflicts and potential conflicts are the most frequent and usually the easiest of the three types to resolve. Even these conflicts, however, may not rank with the lowest severity.

There is a fourth type of conflict you may have experienced in your dreams. In these situations, the entire conflict takes place in your unconscious. You will be totally unaware of these conflicts and what they entail. Therefore, you will be unaware of any responsibility. The unconscious alone will detect a conflict and attempt to communicate the problem to your conscious mind. You will think everything is OK until you suddenly experience a negative prophecy dream. These conflicts are not resolvable.

Besides frequency, each conflict must be evaluated separately for its relative importance. While recurring conflicts with high emotion are always the most important, you also have to consider how long you have had the conflict. The longer you have had a problem, the harder it is to solve. Is this conflict critical to your life? Does it affect your most important relationships or career? While no conflict is easy, the better defined, more recent, and less emotional it is, the easier it will be to handle. Your creative, conscious mind is in charge of conflict resolution techniques. Only the general support of your unconscious is needed.

If you expect success, you will be successful. Once you become familiar with the opening up process and have experienced positive results, you can move up to more difficult conflicts. To get started, we are going to begin with one-time conflicts. After selecting the most unemotional and harmless conflict, open your conflict file, and give the conflict a unique name.

Then, as precisely as you can, define both the ideal and the negative urge involved.

Reinforcement Technique

The first technique is a simple reinforcement of the superior ideal under attack. We do not need to involve the inferior, emotional, unconscious side of a harmless, one-time conflict. This approach works well with low emotional conflicts, and it is also useful in supporting low-emotion dream awareness suggestions. While this is a very simple technique, it still requires planning and creativity. Reinforcement is also an easy way to obtain quick benefits. You are going to perform a little theatrical ceremony that uses your creative imagination to get the attention of your unconscious. The perfect reinforcement action combines physical action with all your senses and uses a symbolic object. While the action must be very short, honest, pertinent, and direct, it must be performed seriously and deliberately. Do not turn this simple reinforcement ceremony into a big deal. Your attitude during the activity should be, "I am doing this to remind myself that this ideal is important to me." Give no thought to the conflict itself.

Example of a Basic Conflict

The following sample conflict is based upon a father's guilt about working late and spending less time with his child than he thinks he should. This is a common conflict we usually tolerate without addressing. As you have learned, however, even small conflicts have their consequences. A simple ceremony provided an effective resolution by gaining the attention and assistance of his unconscious.

The Ceremony

The short and effective ceremony he chose was taking one of the child's toys to his office before work and installing it, with respect, next to his inbox. He did this while thinking about the child. This ceremony took only a minute to perform, but the physical act made a powerful symbolic statement to his unconscious. After this simple act of reinforcement, he felt the positive effects every time he saw the toy and thought about it. He was able to use the new, positive energy he felt to do something good for himself and his child.

In summary, your goal in such a conflict is to reinforce your challenged but still intact ideal. It requires a private ritual that contains four elements: emotion, physical action, an appropriate setting, and symbolism. The ceremony says symbolically to the unconscious that your ideal is being honored and reinforced in this specific place. We want our unconscious to agree with us. Be prepared to repeat the ceremony from time to time. Remember, some conflicts never go away.

Be Careful

Never perform any ceremony by reenacting a dream, and never act out a fantasy dream, even in jest. Reenacting a collective unconscious dream can be dangerous. Remember that suggestions in awareness dreams are only suggestions. You should use your dream content only to get ideas. You must design your own imaginative ceremonies while being careful not to reenact the dream itself.

Bridge Technique

I call the second technique "bridging." This approach works well in low to medium emotional conflicts. Bridging is especially effective when you have two ideals in conflict or when the conscious and unconscious disagree on the solution to a problem. Bridging always involves reinforcing the superior ideal in a new, highly valued partnership with the complementary aspects of the inferior value.

Example of an Intermediate Conflict

You are working two full-time jobs and supporting your family by working seven days a week. The emotional conflict is that you are dreaming about running away and having the fun in your life you deserve. Ignoring your emotional need for fun is no longer an option. You are feeling tense all day long from being overworked, and you are having trouble controlling your emotions.

We all understand this conflict. Do we give in to our unconscious demands to have fun, and if so, how much fun are we entitled to? Think of a dream character called "fun" living inside your unconscious mind. He is full of anger and resentment, and you cannot ignore him anymore. If you give in to his urge for escape and fun, he may think he is more important than supporting your family. This will create even more conflict in your dreams. Don't forget, each urge is a single purpose entity and must be dealt with individually. By understanding the wisdom behind your unconscious urge to have fun, you may be able to bridge the conflict.

Find Common Ground for the Bridge

In this case, the inferior urge to have fun may be turned into a positive. After all, you need some fun in your life to be emotionally healthy, and you need to be healthy in order to continue to support your family. Part of the inferior urge reinforces your superior ideal. Do not for a moment think this approach is a clever trick to fool your unconscious. You cannot trick your unconscious. A bridge strategy must use the true wisdom of the unconscious to support your values and ideals. The bridge approach, if well thought-out, has short-term and long-term positive effects on your unconscious.

In this case, you first need to find something truly fun that has the secondary benefit of keeping you healthy. Secondly, make a personal commitment to partake in the fun activity regularly for some minimum amount of time. You are, in effect, bargaining with your unconscious character, "fun." You exchange two hours a week in fun martial arts training, and "fun" helps you stay healthy and work two jobs.

The last step is to design a reinforcement ceremony centering on your new commitment to fun, health, and financial responsibility. This may take a lot of thought and imagination. Don't forget the four required elements: emotion, physical action, an appropriate setting, and symbolism.

You could hold a three-minute, private sunrise service where you wear your new fighting shorts, kick your feet in the air, smile a lot, hold your gym contract in your hand, and think about how important it is to have fun and be healthy for a change. Make a nonverbal commitment to yourself to set aside time for fun, and thank your unconscious fun character for keeping you healthy so you can support your family.

Don't Renege on Your Promises

Whatever you decide, it must be authentic and make sense. You cannot just promise to do something healthy and fun. You have to follow through with the commitment. It also has to really be fun and not just healthy. If it stops being fun, find something else right away that is fun. Long-term success comes from working with your unconscious while staying true to your values.

The Double Bridge Technique

The third technique I call "double bridging." If you have an irresolvable conflict with your unconscious due to an ethical dilemma, it is worth trying this approach. I find it very effective in most moderate conflicts, but it needs reinforcement from time to time. The technique involves reinforcing your superior ideal with a complementary, tangential ideal, which is associated with but different from the urge you must reject for ethical reasons. Sometimes this technique also works in recurring, high-emotion conflicts.

Our collective unconscious can become downright unreasonable, filling us with the urge to do something we simply do not want. When an urge calls us to do something unethical, immoral, or distasteful, before we reject it out of hand, we need to spend time understanding why the conflict is happening. The answer is not obvious because our primitive urges are overly dramatic and exaggerated. To understand the root cause, you need to ignore the emotion, and look for the secondary benefits of giving into the urge. If you can find a useful benefit to the urge, you can usually bridge the conflict as described above. However, if you cannot bridge a strong emotional conflict, you may have to reject the urge in order to bring the matter to an end. Unfortunately, rejecting your unconscious outright is not usually an effective way to quiet its strong opinions. I would give the following method a try once or even twice.

Example of a Complicated Conflict

Consider the following situation. You have received a subpoena to testify against your employer in a legal matter. You see yourself ideally as an honest person and want to testify to the truth. You have already decided to be truthful in your testimony regardless of the likely negative consequences. You also know it will ruin your career, lifestyle, and economic future.

You believe the inner conflict comes from your need to maintain self-control. The benefit of always maintaining self-control is to curb what you want today in exchange for an important future benefit. In this case, however, you cannot exercise self-control without any expectation but punishment. This is made even more difficult because you expect lingering regret and negative consequences for many years to come.

Do Your Research

Let's identify all the positive benefits of giving into your unwanted urge. Intuitively we can identify many. Next, define exactly why it is unethical and morally wrong for you to do so. We also understand those answers very clearly. There is no available bridge. The next step takes a little research. Look up the definition of self-control, and write it down. Don't forget, self-control means two things: voluntary self-restraint and a future benefit.

Find a Similar Ideal Without Conflict

Now comes the interesting part. Double up on your superior ideal. What is another strong ideal that is supportive of honesty and also benefits from something close to self-control? In this case, courage is a superior ideal, and one that is absolutely necessary to tell the truth publicly under oath. Courage also meets our double bridge requirement because voluntary self-restraint over your fear of economic loss is required in order to be courageous in giving truthful testimony. Only the future benefit of self-control is missing. So how do we design our double bridge?

Perform a Complicated Ceremony

This approach requires a more elaborate and slightly longer ceremony as well as an honest narrative. First you must reinforce the double superior ideals. Then reject the conflicting urge giving the specific "ethical" reason. State how you need great courage to reinforce the superior ideal, and ask for the voluntary self-restraint necessary to be courageous. Notice that the replacement ideal, self-restraint is very closely related to self-control. Self-restraint is, of course, self-control without the expectation of a future benefit.

Creative Solution

How can you perform this ceremony? Here is one way. In an empty movie theater, before or after a movie, hold a Bible in your right hand. Sit and silently declare with all sincerity, "Hear ye, hear ye. As an honest man, I cannot lie for future benefit, but I will speak courageously against evil and injustice. I need my self-restraint to overcome the fear of personal risk I accept today." Then place a one-dollar bill on the seat, and leave the room.

This example contains all the required elements of a double bridge ceremony. The theater, "hear ye, hear ye," and Bible are all symbolic of the legal "stage." Speaking against injustice despite personal risk reinforces your courage ideal. Notice the use of self-restraint instead of self-control. The effect of the ritual is to make clear to your unconscious that your morals were critically important to your decision, and you could not accommodate both. At the same time, you did show honor for self-restraint, which is a very similar ideal. The symbol of leaving a one-dollar bill indicates you are willing to pay for your beliefs.

This may seem like a lot of work to solve a conflict, but in this case and many like it, the reward is, there will little to no lingering regret for your difficult decision, regardless of the outcome. Here are a few rules to follow in creating your ceremonies. Do not perform ceremonies with either real or imagined people you know. Stick with small, symbolic objects. The ritual must always be completely ethical and in full accord with your values.

After the Release of Conflict

How will I feel after I release my conflict? It depends upon the person. For some, there will be a burst of extraordinary self-confidence, while others will temporarily feel a little overwhelmed by the experience. In both cases, the increased knowledge will ultimately elevate your consciousness and expand your personality. I always suggest using your newfound energy to acquire new skills and talents. Whatever you do, avoid thinking you are more important, powerful, or superior to anyone.

What happens to my conflict after it is resolved? Your conflicts do not completely go away. You have only negotiated a short-term agreement with your unconscious to make peace with your conscious. You did not discover a way to control your unconscious.

The only way to successfully deal with your unconscious is to accept, understand, and work with it. Otherwise your ideals will be in constant jeopardy. Whenever you sense your ideals and feelings are questionable, you can be sure it is about an unconscious conflict. As powerful as the unconscious is, always remember you are the decision-maker and the responsible one.

The Golden Rule of Conflict Resolution

In summary, whenever your ethics and morality are in conflict with powerful unconscious urges, it is always better to focus on reinforcing the good than challenging the bad. Don't forget, difficulties involving your love life, money, sex, power, and business cannot be helped by any of these techniques. Self-control and honesty are just two of the ideals that frequently conflict with each other. In chapter ten, you will learn how to ask your core conscience for help in solving problems based on difficult conflicts of ideals and ethics.

Chapter 10
Opening Up to Your Conscience

Your Amazing Soul

The unquestioned knowledge that man possesses a soul has deep roots in virtually all forms of societies and religions throughout recorded history. From ancient Egypt in four thousand BC to the present, more than 90 percent of the world's religions, including the Baha'i faith, Brahma Kumaris, Tibetan Buddhism, Judaism, Roman Catholicism, Orthodox Christianity, Eastern Orthodox, Oriental Orthodox, Protestantism, Seventh-day Adventists, Jehovah's Witnesses, Church of the Latter Day Saints, Hinduism, Islam, Jainism, Sikhism, and Taoism, have incorporated a belief in the soul. Besides religion, it can be found entrenched in the world history of philosophy, literature, poetry, and art. Modern scientists agree that an intuitive belief in an inner spirit is a universal characteristic of man. While the existence of an inner spirit, also known as the soul, cannot be explained by either biological or cultural beliefs, we intuitively know it is real.

The Voice of the Conscience

Besides having a God image, we also have an inner voice associated with the soul within our core. The voice speaks frequently in our dreams with enlightened spiritual and moral authority. It functions within our core as an inner conscience. Jung speculated that the awesome archetype of God is within us to make us aware of God living inside of us.

Hearing Voices in Our Dreams Is Normal

The ability to hear voices in our dreams is as natural as seeing phantasms and imaginary characters of all types and shapes within our dreams. If we experienced the same visions and voices while awake, however, we would be having hallucinations. Please do not be concerned when I speak about the voice of your inner conscience. You will not be subject to any form of hallucinations. Hallucinations, by definition, exclude dreams. Even daydreaming and the internal discussions we have with ourselves are perfectly normal. The time for concern is when we begin to talk aloud with ourselves in public or see things that do not exist while awake.

Asking Our Conscience Questions

As part of this chapter, you will be asking your conscience the questions you have been preparing throughout this program. These are the most serious questions that matter deeply to you. You honestly do not know the answers.

You will be asking your conscience questions using the same technique you have been using to remember your dreams. For many weeks now, you have been communicating with your core by using suggestions spoken silently in the transition between being awake and asleep.

The technical description of drowsiness before sleep is being "hypnagogic," while "hypnopompic" describes being half awake. A common phenomenon associated with both quasi-dream states is hearing the voice of the inner conscience.

Just as you have been asking your core to assist in remembering your dreams, you will now use the same technique to ask your conscience well-thought out questions. Within a few days of asking, you will receive your response either by a dream or by hearing the voice of your conscience as you awaken. This is quite an extraordinary experience.

You Will Not Hear the Voice of God

Please do not expect to hear the voice of God in this program. You may have a long history of praying to God for direct help in your life, and you may have received what you believe to be divine help. Until now, however, you never had the expectation of hearing the voice of God. Do not start now. I do not believe it is possible to hear God outside of a highly exceptional numinous dream, which is beyond the scope of this book.

The Voice of the Conscience Is Familiar

The voice of your conscience, the voice you will soon hear, is already familiar to you. It functions as your personal moral guide. It may points you toward your God image but the voice is not God's.

Whether you believe in God or not does not change the reality of the inner conscience and how it functions. All you need to answer your most difficult questions is to "ask and you will receive, search and you will find, knock and the door will be opened for you."

How to Ask Your Question

Let's focus on asking your conscience a specific question. It must be appropriate, short, clear, and respectful. The only rule is your question must help you become a better person. Philosophical, moral, or conflict questions are always appropriate. In truth, I do not know which specific questions will be answered and which will not. You can always ask for helpful knowledge. Provided the question is appropriate, it will be answered. You cannot ask your conscience what stock to buy, if you will marry the subject of your love, or whether you should get divorced.

The principal limitation of this bedtime technique is that the question must be reduced to a short sentence. Many of your questions will be complicated and, therefore, a challenge to summarize. Your newly enhanced relationship with your unconscious, however, will make the process much easier. Over time, you will become proficient in distilling the details into an abstracted question. By thinking about the details while you ask the question, the full message will successfully transmit.

Keep It Short and Precise

The question must precisely state what you want to know. If you ask the question incorrectly, you will get the right answer to the wrong question. The question must not contain a negative such as, "because I don't want" or, "how do I not." The unconscious does not understand the use of negatives. Just as your dreams do not contain negatives, your questions cannot either.

How you ask someone a question also affects the answer you receive. Your inner conscience is no different. Your conscience is not God. It does not have to be addressed with fear. It does, however, need to be treated with the same courtesy and respect as a loving friend. The question cannot command or demand an answer. It should not include any doubt that it will be answered. It must be a request for help that allows your conscience to decide whether to answer or not.

What Does My Conscience Sound Like?

You probably are wondering what the voice of your conscience will sound like. I am sure you have already heard the voice in your dreams, but you may not remember. I can only speak about my own experience. My voice is distant but also clear, supremely confident, and only slightly below midrange male. My conscience is simultaneously brilliant, eloquent, autonomous, fearless, honest, direct, compassionate, protective, and very humorous. It speaks in a distinctive rhetorical style that always ends with an unexpected punch line. As for my personal experiences, however, I must claim privacy as you must as well.

The answer from your conscience always contains a larger-than-self and non-self viewpoint of what is "good" for you. That knowledge and understanding can psychologically change your moral imperatives. It will speak of universal truths from a higher authority than your highest motives and values.

You will soon receive special knowledge from your core conscience in your dreams. While you do not have to obey your conscience, you may feel uncomfortable if you do not. The actions advocated by your conscience are clearly independent and not your own. As opposed to collective urges that feel essentially visceral, the voice of the conscience can create moral understanding that stops us in our tracks. We may find we simply cannot do what we wanted or intended to do.

If You Are Ready, Do It Tonight

If you are ready to ask your question tonight, instead of saying your dream suggestion, simply insert your question in its place. Make sure you are finished with your intentions and that this question is your last thought before sleep. Remember to breathe in slowly while asking the question, and exhale slowly while saying the numbers from ten to zero (skipping the number eight). Think about the question while you repeat the series of repetitions at least five times before falling asleep.

Don't be upset if nothing happens after the first night. It frequently takes a few days to receive an answer. It almost always takes a few days to answer a complicated question. Don't stop asking. If you are patient, and the question meets the criteria, you will receive an answer in time. There is truth in the old saying, "we do not find our soul; our soul finds us." Answers from your conscience are your well-deserved reward for your core work and becoming a more "complete" person.

You Are Responsible

Despite receiving the most appropriate, valuable, and moral knowledge from your conscience, you are still responsible for your actions. You cannot ever make a choice based solely upon any part of your unconscious, including knowledge from your conscience and/or a powerful numinous dream complete with the voice of God. Your unconscious mind, just like your conscious mind, is subject to corruption and malfunction in ways we do not understand. The primitive unconscious of man has been known to twist truth into clever lies by innumerable means, including seductive moral traps intended to promote immoral purposes. It will always take conscious intelligence and strong courage to make your difficult decisions.

How Can You Be Sure the Voice Is Your Conscience?

As you already know, not every voice you hear in a dream state is your conscience. That raises the question, how can you tell if the voice is really your inner conscience? The answer requires some experience and a good amount of common sense.

After you have heard the voice of your conscience a few times, it will become more familiar and identifiable. You will look forward to hearing the distinctive clarity, meter, and tone of that waking voice. If it ever presents differently in any way, you should be highly suspicious.

After you review and think about a conscience message, you need to be intuitive. How do you feel in your gut? Does the message make you feel good, even if you disagree with what it says? Would the answer bring about the highest good in you? Did the message increase your understanding? Answers that lead to fixations, fantasies, feeling bad about yourself, wanting to control others, or doing unethical things, even temporarily for a common future good, are not coming from your conscience.

I believe strongly in the old saying, "we know the tree by its fruit." Look carefully and skeptically at what you experience. Your conscience is benign. It will not harm you. It knows what is good for you. On receiving my first message, I smiled with happiness for days.

Your Conscience in Your Dreams

Dreams with the appearance of your conscience are very common. Your conscience can appear in many forms, but most commonly, it appears as a person usually described as a "wise, old man." Besides participating in your everyday awareness and prophecy dreams, this wise man will typically appear to miraculously solve an insolvable problem that has been bothering you. While psychologists and psychiatrists report that the conscience can also appear as a young boy, a dwarf, a beautiful woman, or even an animal, that has not been my experience.

After you receive your response from your conscience, I suggest you acknowledge it with a simple ceremony. Think of it as a thank-you card.

Congratulations on completing *Finding Our Purpose in Life.* The program has put you in the center of your own life, so whenever you face doubt or confusion, you can always respond without fear. While thinking is hard work and takes time, there is no substitute for it in decision-making. Do not fear your emotions. Acknowledge them, live with them, and put them to work in positive actions.

This book was designed to give you the minimum skills and experience to open up to your core. If you find you enjoyed the subject of your beneficial core and wish to know more about it, a lengthy reading list can be found in the appendix, including the primary source material I used in writing this book.

Save Your Work

There is no requirement that you continue logging your dreams. I keep my recorder next to my bed in the event I have an important dream. I automatically process all my dreams mentally and review only the most important ones. Whatever you do, save all your hard work. As long as it is encrypted or kept in a safe place, your secrets are safe. You will have situations in the future where your past work will be invaluable. Due to your training, you will now sense new conflicts long before they turn into big trouble. The longer you ignore conflicts, the more difficult they are to resolve.

Your Purpose in Life

Now you have opened up to your core, you have a lot of new mental energy at your disposal. The feeling can be intoxicating. Please realize you did not receive these feelings as a reward from your core for all your hard work. All you have done is reacquire the mental energy you have been squandering in the past. You are not a more superior person than when you started. The only thing superior about you now is that you know you are not superior.

If you start thinking you deserve this temporary high, it will be gone in a week or two, and you will feel terrible. Your relationship with your core needs to be ongoing to keep you in balance. How you feel now is how you are supposed to feel all the time. You want to get used to the feeling.

I strongly suggest you use your new energy to fulfill the true purpose of your life. I want you to go back to chapter seven, and look again at the ideal projection of yourself. Some of your ideals will relate to character, while others will relate to life situations, including work, home, and parenting. It is your action ideals, however, that describe your true hidden purpose. This is who you were born to become. These are the goals that will give meaning to your life. This is your life quest. Taken collectively, all your higher ideals and values should combine to make up your true-life story. Don't squander your energy by inflating your self-importance. While our ideals are important, we must never forget it is the *benefit* of our ideals we are really after. Always focus on the benefits and not the ideals.

Please use your new energy to be the person you were born to become. It will never be easier to achieve than today. The alignment of your core with your ideals and best motivations has already provided you with greater purpose and meaning. By successfully living out your life quest in harmony with your positive core, you will ascend to an even higher level of core awareness.

You have done magnificent work. Keep working together with your ideals. This way, you and your core will reach the next level and beyond.

On August 6, 2011 I had reconstructive surgery at Georgetown University Hospital in Washington, DC to resect my impacted major and minor occipital nerves. The operation was a great success! I have not had a single "lie on the floor" headache ever since. Thankfully, my waking dream songs have continued to this day.

Bibliography

1. Almoli, S. *Dream Interpretation*. (Hoboken: KTAV Publishing House, 1998).

2. Augusto, L. M. "Unconscious Knowledge: A Survey," *Advances in Cognitive Psychology* 6 (2010): 116–41.

3. Etkin, A., Klemenhagen, K., Dudman, J., Rogan, M., Hen, R. and E. Kandel. "Individual Differences in Trait Anxiety Predict the Response of the Basolateral Amygdala to Unconsciously Processed Fearful Faces." *Neuron* 44 (2004): 1043-55

4. Hannah, B. *Encounters with the Soul*. (Wilmette: Chiron Publications, 1981).

5. Johnson, R. A. *Inner Work*. (New York: HarperCollins Publishers, 1986).

6. Jung, C. G. *Civilization in Transition*. (Princeton: Princeton University Press, 1964).

7. Jung, C. G. *Four Archetypes*. (Princeton: Princeton University Press, 1959).

8. Jung, C. G. *Jung on Evil*. (Princeton: Princeton University Press, 1995).

9. Jung, C. G. *On the Nature of the Psyche*. (Princeton: Princeton University Press, 1960).

10. Jung, C. G. *The Psychology of the Transference*. (Princeton: Princeton University Press, 1954).

11. Jung, C. G. *The Red Book*. (New York: W. W. Norton & Company, 2009).

12. Jung, C.G. *The Undiscovered Self* (Boston: Little, Brown and Company, 1957).

13. Laughlin, T. *Jungian Psychology*. Vol. 2. (Los Angeles: Panarion Press, 1982).

14. Milner, A. D. and M. A. Goodale. "Two Visual Systems Reviewed," *Neuropsychologia* 33 (2007): 1117–30.